CALIFORNIA COWBOYS

In the land of big hats and long horns.

(Photograph by Dane Coolidge)

California
COWBOYS

DANE COOLIDGE

With Photographs by the Author

THE UNIVERSITY OF ARIZONA PRESS
Tucson, Arizona

About the Author

DANE COOLIDGE (1873–1940) was an itinerant photographer and writer who traveled throughout the American West, recording native wildlife and the developing frontier. He was the author of numerous magazine pieces and books, perhaps the best known of which are *Arizona Cowboys, Texas Cowboys,* and *Old California Cowboys.*

Originally published as
Old California Cowboys

Copyright, 1939 by E. P. Dutton & Co., Inc.
Copyright renewed 1967
by Coit Coolidge and Mrs. Calvin Gaines Collins
All Rights Reserved

THE UNIVERSITY OF ARIZONA PRESS
First Printing 1985
Manufactured in the U.S.A.

Library of Congress Cataloging in Publication Data

Coolidge, Dane, 1873–1940.
California cowboys.

Reprint. Originally published: Old California cowboys.
New York : Dutton, 1939.
1. Cowboys—California—History. 2. Cowboys—Arizona—
History. 3. Cowboys—Mexico—Sonora (State)—History.
4. California—Social life and customs. 5. Arizona—
Social life and customs. 6. Sonora (Mexico : State)—
Social life and customs.   I. Title.
F866.C76   1985   979.1   84-28001

ISBN 0-8165-0862-3

Contents

Illustrations

Illustrations

ONE: COWBOYS IN CALIFORNIA

Chapter I

THE CALIFORNIANS

WITHIN a few years after 1769, when Portolá brought the first cattle into California, the fertile valleys from San Diego to San Francisco became a cowman's paradise. The stock ran wild, increasing so rapidly that every vaquero had a horse to ride and beef to broil by the fire. Both were free for the asking to any man with Spanish blood in his veins and, while the Indians around the missions raised corn and beans, the Californians lived like gentlemen.

Let the neophytes and Mexican peons do the work in the field. *They* were Spanish *caballeros,* the true nobility, who never soiled their hands with humble toil but stepped up on their horses at dawn. In their language a horseman and a gentleman were the same, and an unmounted man was a slave. The *gente de razon* were a class by themselves, spending their time in fiestas and social pleasures, gambling and racing, and deeds of prowess on horseback.

They lived simply on beef and beans, corn tortillas and coffee, and their white adobe houses were given over to festivities, at which they drank their native wine. To make it easier to catch their horses every mount dragged a rawhide rope, and the first thing in the morning one was brought up and tied outside the guest's door. If there was a dance or fiesta within

11

forty miles—and there usually was—a party must be arranged and all ride off for the day—or the week; time was nothing to them.

From San Francisco to San Diego there was not a single hotel or inn but every twenty miles along the Camino Real, there stood a mission and a town, and to whichever house a man went he was received as a welcome guest. If his horse was tired out they gave him another one, he was fed and entertained and urged to stay and, in case he had had bad luck at the monte games, in every spare room a pile of guest-silver was laid out, to speed him on his way. It was a point of honor with those early Californians never to count the money that was left.

Young ladies rode in front on the saddle, gallantly supported by some gay *caballero*, who occupied the crupper behind. Nor were the women lacking in that proud horsemanship which was the sign of their aristocratic blood. They even rode out on the bear-hunts and, with pistols, helped to kill fierce grizzlies. Wild bulls and grizzly bears were dragged into the arena where, while youth and beauty looked on, they were tied together by the feet and left to fight it out.

To celebrate some wedding they would dance all night for a week, only stealing a few hours off to make up a little sleep. There were barrels of native wine and the fiery *aguardiente*, which brought on many a knife fight; and all was music and song and old-world hospitality. In the earliest days Manila galleons brought over silks and fine fabrics from the

A Matanza.
Killing cattle for the hides and tallow.
(*From Vischer's Pictorial of California*)

GRIZZLY BEAR HUNT IN SOUTHERN CALIFORNIA.
Showing the long hair and fancy costumes of the early Californians.
(From Vischer's Pictorial of California)

Orient, and when Yankee traders came to buy hides they enjoyed the greatest splendor in the world—while it lasted.

At last the Californians had a market for the thousands of fat cattle which ran in the hills half wild; and in great *matanzas* they slaughtered them with the knife, leaving the skinning for the base peons. Men on horseback dashed through the herds, killing the animals with one blow in the neck, after which the hides were stripped off and the fat tried out for tallow. Then, while the sailors loaded their ships for the long voyage around the Horn, the supercargoes spread out the luxuries of the Indies and the Spaniards bought and bought.

It was not how much but how good, with them, and as the years went on and the traffic increased the traders brought the best they could find. Chinese silks and damasks, delicate laces and hand-wrought stuffs, Spanish embroideries and French tapestries; and, for the men, the most gorgeous costumes that horsemen ever devised. It was not enough that a saddle should be silver-mounted, stamped in red and green and gold. The rider must be dressed in blue and red velvet, his pantaloons slashed down the sides to display the white linen beneath, his deerskin leggings fastened with jewels.

His flat-topped sombrero followed a round of fashions; but the yellow hat of vicuña skin, imported from Peru, seems to have set the style that stuck. It had a wide rim, the crown encircled with a band of silver or gold braid, fastened with a jewelled pin. And for a belt he wore a sash of silk, carrying his knife inside his right legging. Any space left over was decorated with silver buttons, embroidered frogs and Spanish laces, made by his lady fair. He wore his hair long, had a small black moustache, and, over all, a cloak of blue or black broadcloth which stamped him for what he was—a gentleman.

But when he stepped up on a horse he was more than that—a *caballero, muy jinete*. Nor was it a pose, a grand opera effect, for these Californians could ride. They spent their lives in the saddle, travelling always at a gallop except when slowed down to a walk, and when it came to equestrian sports they had some rough-and-ready stunts that are unbelievable now. I have never known a cowboy who could get his horse up to a bear, to say nothing of putting a rope on one. But when they wanted a little excitement, the Spaniards would catch one lone-handed—rope him and bring him in, to tie his hindfoot to the forefoot of a bull and let them fight it out.

That is no boy's play, at any age or time; and, when they felt real bravo, one would step down off his horse and kill a grizzly bear with his knife. Grizzly Adams, the old bear-tamer, was the only American on record who had the nerve to undertake that—and he had many wounds to show for it. But, with a rawhide shield on the left arm, the Mexicans would advance on foot and kill one without a scratch.

Chapter II

DON FRANCISCO GALLARDO

MUCH has been written of the exploits of those early Spaniards and in the reading it sounds like a fable but, more than thirty years ago, I had the honor of meeting one in the flesh. No less a man than Don Francisco Gallardo, his hair and beard white with the frost of age but strong and active still. On the road past Volcan Mountain in Southern California, while we fought our way up from the Colorado Desert against a sandstorm that had lasted all day, he stepped out suddenly from a rugged pathway and greeted us with a courtly bow. In one hand, like a staff, he carried a miner's drill and from his belt there dangled a huge horn-spoon, sawn from the curve of some mighty horn. A handkerchief, bulging with rocks, completed his outfit and marked him for a prospector, out seeking desert gold.

His worn shoes had been laced over with rawhide *tejuas,* with the hairy side out, the better to cling to the rocks. He stood upright against the storm, bowing with old-world politeness, but as our mules caught the smell of smoke from a ranch-house they hurried on—and we passed him by. Behind us black clouds were fighting their way against the freezing blasts from the north. The imminence of a great storm lay upon the desert and, with every bird and beast, we were running for cover.

But for a fierce caprice of the weather, there would be no record here of Don Francisco Gallardo, the friend of Eduardo Duarte and Pio Pico, a lawyer who in his day had defended the Castros and General Vallejo and lived on terms of intimacy with all the Spanish gentlemen in California.

But when we awoke in the morning the air was thick with falling snow and all the outside world was white. For the first time in twenty years the mesquites along the edge of the desert were bowed beneath the weight of snow, and from above the soft flakes sifted down endlessly, filling us all with wonder. And in the barn, coiled up in a bundle of hay like a mouse in its winter nest, we came upon Gallardo, too proud to ask himself into the house. He insisted that he slept in the cold on the advice of his physician, but we easily induced him to come in and get warm.

Sitting behind the stove, the old man ate ravenously, slyly loosening his belt when no one was looking; and when he could hold no more, he leaned back and began a story. It was the first of many, of which he was always the hero—tales of loves and hidden treasure, of legal battles where the fate of Spanish grants hung in the balance, and feats of skill and strength. And, to make sure that he forgot nothing, he referred often to a roll of onionskin paper, written on both sides, and

16

across on both sides, giving the names and dates of each occurrence.

What a wealth of early history that roll contained! But in three days he had disappeared from our ken, leaving only a fragmentary memory.

"I am old," he said, drawing closer to the fire, "and yet I am a better man than many a youth in his prime. I well remember the time when the Pueblo de Los Angeles was little more than a country village and with my good horse, Chapuli—which in Spanish means The Grasshopper—I was the greatest rider of them all. With the exception of my good friend, Don Eduardo Duarte; and it was to get the use of my wonderful mount that he took me, a young boy, into his confidence.

"And to be the friend of Don Eduardo was to sit at the right hand of a king. Yet a jester, too, for when he had lost all his money at monte, even cutting the silver buttons off his coat, he would go out on the open plains, where the horses were running wild, and catch one with a rope—a slender *reata* which he used to support his pantaloons and therefore could not gamble away; and when the people saw him riding one off, they would laugh and say: 'It is only Eduardo Duarte.'

"But how he could catch those wild horses in the open no one knew, till he told it to me. In those early days the grizzly bears were very plentiful, and when they wanted to kill a horse they would lie on their backs in a grassy place and throw their huge legs in the air, to attract the inquisitive herds. Then, when they came close, the bear would jump to his feet and, before they could escape, he would strike one down with his paw.

"It was from watching these bears that Don Eduardo first learned to lure some fine horse up close, until, with his slender *reata*, he would cast his *lazo*, spring astride and ride away. Only fifteen years ago, when I sorely needed the money, I earned twenty-five dollars by using this trick in catching a magnificent black mule; but first I must tell you about Don Eduardo and the feats of horsemanship he performed.

"The greatest of these was to jump a wild bull over a gate made of seven bars; and, as he went over, the rider would follow so close behind that he would seize it by the tail and, taking his turns around the horn, throw the bull on its head and break its neck. This feat was performed at the end of some great festival, when many people were looking on. The *caballeros*, dividing into two parties, would rush some bull to and fro until, when it became wild with rage, one party or the other would head it toward the gate and, as it leapt over, some great horseman like Eduardo Duarte would jump his horse up beside it and throw the bull on its head.

"But of all the horses in the Pueblo de Los Angeles there was none equal to my noble mount, Chapuli, when it came to leaping over bars; and after we were pursued by a terrible grizzly bear he became famous all over California. In the river bottom below the town there was a pasture where our best horses were kept, and to protect them from wild animals a high fence was built. Yet, even over that, Chapuli could jump; and by doing so he saved my life.

"For an enormous grizzly bear, nearly ten feet in height, had got inside the fence and, hiding in the heavy willows, he struck down every horse that passed. Several men had been killed in battles with this animal, called the Terrible Bear of Los Angeles; and at last, when no one would enter the *potrero*, I offered to ride around and open the further gate, to let the remaining horses escape.

"It was almost sundown and I was returning to the pueblo when, from the willows ahead, I saw his head appear, and my horse began to snort. But I spoke to him softly and he kept on down the road until, nearing the spot where the terrible bear was hiding, I suddenly leaned forward in my saddle and shouted: 'Santiago!'

"That is the war cry always used by the Spaniards when they charged against the Moors—referring to St. James, the protector of the Catholic faith—and it was also used to start a horse race, all our steeds being trained for war. So, when I shouted 'Santiago' my noble horse sprang forward and, before the terrible bear could break out of his hiding place, we passed him.

"Off we went down the road, and no one would believe how fast the grizzly came behind us; but when Chapuli sensed the bear he ran like the wind, and so we came to the gate. It was made of seven bars, with a bull-hide hung over it, and here the bear thought to catch us, but Chapuli leaped over it as lightly as a bird, for he was accustomed to the sport of the seven bars, called in Spanish, *colear*. I heard a great crash as the bear ran against it and, before he could climb over, we were far down the road, though in the distance I could still see him coming.

"Now on the outskirts of the town, where the frightened inhabitants were in hiding, there was a leaning cottonwood which was used to rope horses from above and, leaving my horse, I borrowed an *escopeta*, or musket, and ran back to climb up the tree. Just before dark I heard a grunting below me and felt the tree trunk tremble. It was the terrible bear, which many thought was possessed of a devil; but I waited till I could see his teeth clearly, then shot him in the mouth. He fell dead and that night all the people trooped out, to do honor to the man who had killed him.

"But that was long ago, before the Americans came, seizing the lands of the Californians, dispossessing them of all they owned. In my profession as an attorney at law, I worked day and night, trying to save something for them from the wreck, but the Spanish

20

records were very defective and so nearly everything was lost. I remember the sad case of a very wealthy Spaniard, one of the richest men in the State. When he died I was sent for by the widow and when I asked if she had kept any papers she brought out everything she had.

"Being very poorly educated she had taken old pillow-slips and put into them every paper she got. Whether it was a deed for thousands of acres of land or a bill for some butcher's meat it made no difference to her, but after sorting them all over, I got the papers ready and she promised to have them recorded. That was all that was necessary to establish her right to the property, but on the way to the county seat the driver of the livery team persuaded her to stop and marry him. He had been bribed by the land-grabbers to make this alliance and when they came to the Courthouse, he refused to sign the deeds. Of all ignorant people an ignorant woman is the worst; and, while trying to save her, I neglected my own affairs until I was left with almost nothing.

"It was in the month of February, 1886, when from the stress of legal work a sickness came over me which the doctors could not cure. I was, moreover, in straitened circumstances and, while there were men who owed me thousands of dollars, I had hardly enough to pay my landlady. It was a season also of incessant rains which kept me to my room; and so the Spring came on until, one day while I was still weak from my fever, the sun burst out upon us suddenly and the longing to get away overcame me.

"Without telling anybody of my intentions, I left the house and went to the pasture where my glorious horse Juan was kept; and when he saw me he came galloping along the fence, eager to take the trail. But the keeper would by no means deliver him to me until I paid the pasturage, which I lacked the money to do. So I went home and considered and, since it is no part of a Spanish gentleman to demand money of those who owe him, I borrowed twenty-five dollars from an old friend, promising to repay him soon, and early the next morning I set off.

"That was indeed a perfect morning, when we galloped out the road that leads from Alameda. In my great gladness to be free I had no care in the world and at every crossroad I threw the reins on my horse's neck. But always he turned his head to the south and I could see that he remembered the Arroyo Hondo, near the valley that is now called Livermore. In the old days we had stopped there for several months while I was recovering from the bite of a huge grizzly, which we had encountered in the higher mountains. And, since we were on the adventure together, I allowed him to lead the way; but in my own mind I was considering how I could repay the twenty-five dollars which my friend Mr. Severance had given me.

"At last we came to the gate of the old ranch in the

Arroyo Hondo and the gentleman who now owned the place, a Mr. Barlow, very courteously invited me to dinner. Throughout the meal I had observed that he was regarding me curiously and as I went out to care for my horse he followed after me.

" 'I notice,' he said, 'that you have a very good *reata* on your saddle. May I ask if you are skilled in the throwing of the lasso?'

" 'As for that,' I replied, 'I am an old man, and my horse is fresh from pasture, but in my younger days I could throw the *lazo* with the best of them!'

" 'Very good,' he said, 'now listen to me. I have in my hillside pasture a black mule, for which I am offered two hundred dollars delivered; and yet I am unable to conquer him, for he is as fierce as any wild beast and will not allow another animal in the pasture. Several months ago I sent to San Jose for the best three vaqueros in that town, but after they had caught him and fastened him with a long rope he tore the heavy post from the ground and ran back, wilder than ever.

" 'And even when I offered them double the money they would not undertake his recapture, for now wherever he ran he trailed the great stake after him, and their horses were afraid to approach. For two months I have offered a reward of twenty-five dollars to any man who will rope and tie this devil, and if he is not captured soon I shall be obliged to shoot him, for he deprives me of the use of the whole pasture.'

"Now all this was good news to me, and I already

counted the money as good as won, so without more words I followed Mr. Barlow to the pasture. There we found the mule, a magnificent creature as black as night; and when he saw us he galloped back and forth, snorting and dragging his great stake as if it were a mustard stalk.

" 'Do you think you can catch that animal?' asked Mr. Barlow.

" 'That I promise you,' I replied, 'but it cannot be done in a day.'

" 'A week or a month!' he cried, 'it is nothing to me, so long as you catch him. When he is safely tied to the snubbing post I will pay you the reward in gold, and until then you shall be my guest.'

"So on the very first day my horse Juan brought me to an adventure, and I would have fulfilled my promise at once except that I wished to be alone. The day being Thursday I waited therefore until Sunday, when Mr. Barlow and his wife would be at church, and no sooner had they departed for town than I went about my task, the secret of which I had learned from my old friend, Eduardo Duarte.

"Of all the vaqueros in the Pueblo de Los Angeles, Don Eduardo was by far the best, and at taming wild horses he had no equal. If he had a fault it was gaming, and often he lost both horse and saddle at the gambling booths; yet he was never compelled to walk, for, as I told you, he had the secret of enticing the wildest horses within his throw; after which he would

24

ride off unmolested, for he was greatly beloved by everyone.

"There were many, indeed, who wondered by what means Don Eduardo approached these wild horses, but he would never tell. Yet at last out of friendship he told me, and it was this same device which I now prepared to use, to lure the black mule up so close that I could cut the stake loose from his rope.

"The pasture where the black mule ranged was long and open, rising to a hill upon one side and running into a deep marsh upon the other—an evil place indeed for roping and throwing. Stripping off my outer clothes, and armed only with a sharp hatchet, I crept along the upper fence to the brow of the hill, where I lay hidden until my disguise was perfected. My hair and beard I rumpled till they stood up like the mane of a lion and my face was almost concealed. On a short stick I tied my handkerchief and, lying upon the hillside, I thrust it between my legs and out behind, where I waved it like a tail.

"Then, clad only in my red underwear, I began to roll and tumble down the hill, bellowing and wagging my tail like some great animal; and when the black mule saw me he ran the length of the pasture and back, snorting like mad. So blinded was he by terror that all thought of deceit was driven from his mind, yet the fascination of curiosity would not permit him to stay away. As I rolled upon the open ground he dashed in closer, pawing the earth, and then in sudden panic turned short and scampered away.

"This he repeated several times, coming closer each time, and when I perceived that he was becoming bolder I began to leap about and struggle, making strange outcries, until the hair stood up on his neck in amazement. After each fresh outburst he rushed away in great fear, dragging his stake, and each time I peeped out to see if I could chop it loose with my hatchet.

"Now at last the time had come when I must lure him to me and in a desperate paroxysm I fell upon my face, simulating death. My groans became weaker and weaker; I wagged my tail feebly and let it fall, then with a shudder I lay limp and held my breath.

" 'Pouff!' snorted the black mule, and galloped away like the wind. Instantly I drew the hatchet from my belt and lay watching him as he came thundering back. Once more he crept towards me, his eyes blazing with the fascination of terror. He stretched out his neck to snuff my scent, backing and pawing the ground, and the hair of his fore-top rose up and stood forward between his ears.

"I twitched my hand, and once more he turned to flee, but I leapt to my feet and made after him. Almost at his heels I followed until he overleapt the great stake, and before he could take up the slack and drag it after him I had chopped the rope in two with my hatchet. In like manner my dear friend Eduardo

26

Duarte had feigned death in the pastures, until at last he cast his *reata* about the neck of any horse that he desired. But for the taming of this wild creature I needed the assistance of my horse Juan; and while the black mule stood bewildered I ran to the barn, eager to be after him with the *lazo*.

"In anticipation of success I had planted a heavy snubbing post in the middle of the barnyard and, throwing all the gates wide open, I rode boldly into the pasture. Up and down the wild mule fled before me, but at the first throw I caught him by the neck. It had been my intention to take my turns and throw him, and with that purpose I reined Juan back on his haunches; but no sooner did the mule feel the rope than he wheeled about and charged straight at us, snapping his teeth like a demon from Hades. Never, since the day that I took him from his cruel master, had Juan set his will against mine, but now he plunged and bucked so violently that I was forced to throw loose my *reata* and flee incontinently to the barnyard.

"Here was a pretty outcome to all my scheming! And, the instant he was free, the black devil left off chasing us and plunged straightway into the morass. When at last I rode back into the pasture I saw that the cunning brute had waded to the middle of the marsh and planted himself in the mud so deeply that only his head and ears appeared—and I could swear that as he lay there he opened his mouth and laughed at us. Yet, though he brayed, the battle was not over.

"Speaking gently to my horse I spurred him in, until at last I picked up the end of my *reata;* and, making a *dalavuelta* or Spanish turn about the horn, I jerked sharply on the rope. This I did, thinking to shut off the black mule's breath, but at the first tug he rose up like some fabulous monster and plunged towards us in a storm of mud. Yet, being always upon firmer ground, I had him at a disadvantage; and when we reached dry land I twitched the loop tight in spite of him.

"As, with his coat all plastered with mud, the mule was dragged out, his rage was truly laughable, but the moment he set foot on solid ground the jest quickly turned into earnest. Nay, though Juan was a fast horse and ran like the wind I could hardly keep ahead of him, and we swept into the barnyard like a whirlwind, with the black brute at our heels. From the choking of the rope his eyes stood out like a crab's, but his strength was in no wise abated. I led by the length of my *reata,* but it was nothing more or less than a flight, and the fiery creature snapped his teeth again in expectation of revenge.

"But within the open barnyard my great post stood as solid as its mother oak and, with the mule close after me, I rode past it on the left side. Then, whirling about it as we do in our horse races, I turned sharply to the right, flouting my broad hat in his face. There at last I outwitted him, for, in his blind rage to catch me, he cut across the tangent, passing by on the right side of the post. To meet the shock I spurred Juan forward and, when the rope came taut against the post, it threw the mule in a mighty somersault, flat upon the ground.

"From the jolt of his sudden stop Juan flew back more than a foot and the rawhide twanged like a bowstring; but now at last fortune was with me, for the rope held, and I was quick to follow up my advantage. Before the mule could struggle to his feet I had ridden twice in a great circle about the post, winding my *reata* about its base. Then, leaving Juan to hold the rope taut, I ran with my tying-strings and noosed the mule's forefeet.

"You may well believe I was not long about it and, having been a vaquero, it did not take me long to snare his hind feet and draw all four of them together. When at last Mr. Barlow returned from church I had the pleasure of showing him this wild mule that nobody could approach, nicely hog-tied and fastened to the post.

"As I refused to divulge the manner in which the black mule had been caught, Mr. Barlow upon my departure, offered me ten dollars more for the trick. But this I did not tell him, for we Spaniards in California have little left except our secrets. Yet he took it in good part, and gave me the twenty-five dollars as he had promised.

"So in three days I earned back the money which I owed to my friend, Mr. Severance; and, hearing that much gold was being found along the Tuolumne, I rode there to mend my fortunes. With a young man named Streeter I built a wing-dam to turn the rush of waters aside; and when the stream bed was exposed we found a nugget so heavy that my partner could hardly lift it. From this it seemed certain that our fortune was assured, and as he was a Yankee from Massachusetts who had never seen gold, the young man became perfectly wild.

" 'Only give me this,' he said, 'and you can have all the rest. I *must* have this nugget to take home.'

" 'Very well,' I answered. 'The nugget is yours.'

"But though we went over the bedrock for several days, not another piece of gold could we find. So we parted, still friends, and now after many years I am at last on my way to become rich. Do you see this black rock which I found in the hills only yesterday? Twenty years ago, while on another mission, I noticed this vein along the slope; and it was only last month that, on visiting another mine, I learned that it is nickel. When your partner comes back from hunting deer I know he will recognize it at once."

On account of the heavy snow on the peaks, all the deer in the Volcan Mountains were moving down; and my partner, with our hosts, the two Wilson boys, brought in a buck that night. But they had left two more hung up in a tree where the coyotes would not get them, and the next morning before daylight they were gone. Between hunting and skinning and pack-

ing in the carcasses it was three days before my prospector partner got around to look at the rock.

"That is manganese," he said; and in the dispute
that followed, my old friend's feelings were hurt. The
next morning, when I looked for him in the hay, his
great mouse-nest was empty and Francisco Gallardo
was gone.

Chapter III

THE COMING OF THE GRINGOS

AFTER listening for three days to Gallardo's dissertations on the breaking up of what was really an Empire I began to understand what the Mexican people had suffered in the rush of American land-grabbers. Before the emigrants swarmed in over the mountains and settled on the plains below, the country was given over to cattle-raising; and land, as such, was practically valueless. Any Mexican citizen of good character could acquire for the asking eleven square leagues of land, one capable of irrigation and the others fit for grazing.

It was like the Great Plains when the cattlemen first came in and each man took up a homestead. That one hundred and sixty acres was just a place to live on, a sort of headquarters where they could keep their supplies while they herded their cattle on the prairie. But these settlers from Missouri and the far frontier were boomers, more than home-seekers and farmers. They had come West to get rich, not to make a meager living, and while they were waiting, they took up some land to sell to those who would follow.

But so low did the Mexicans hold their grants that the surveys were often made by men on horseback, one dragging a fifty-foot *reata* at a gallop, while the other kept a rough count. The boundaries were marked by piles of stones, which could be easily knocked down or destroyed; and the records were kept in an equally careless manner, many being entirely lost.

When the Americans rushed in and accurate surveys were called for it was found that in most cases the land originally staked was greatly in excess of that granted. Hence the question came up—which land belonged to the owner or his heirs? Should it be measured from the middle out, or from the outside in, and who was to be the judge? The result of this confusion, and the lack of any adequate land-courts, was that the rough-and-ready Americans simply squatted on any land they wanted.

Even at Sutter's Fort, this great friend of the Americans found himself despoiled of practically all his land, and other possessions as well. He had stocked his leagues of pasture with cattle borrowed from the missions or bought on credit from easygoing Mexicans; and after the discovery of gold there was such a rush of adventurers that the only law was the gun. There was such a wealth of cattle, of land, and of gold that the settlers became drunk with greed.

For many years the series of Franciscan Missions, located a day's journey apart from San Diego to the Golden Gate, had been the centers of agriculture and cattle-raising as well as of hospitality and culture. But, when Mexico revolted against the King of Spain and started a Republic, the Fathers refused to take the oath of allegiance and in 1834 their property was confiscated. Cattle, sheep, and horses were driven off and slaughtered and, when the process of "secularization" was over, many great grants and ranches were well stocked with mission cows.

It was a free-for-all, and if at a later date the Mexicans were stripped of everything, it must be remembered that they in their time had despoiled the thrifty Franciscans. But, now that the missions were abolished and the Indian neophytes "freed," agriculture languished and cattle-raising became almost the only industry. Then began the golden age in California when, by the natural increase of their herds alone, the Mexican rancheros grew rich.

There was no work that they called work to be done. All they had to do was ride around on a good horse and see that their calves were branded. For, early in the settlement, a brand book had been started in which every owner recorded his iron; and at the great rodeos a regularly appointed field judge made sure that the laws were enforced. As the cattle were brought in to the big corrals the vaqueros on their best mounts performed daring feats of horsemanship. Beef was killed to feed the assembled multitude, there was music and gambling and dances, and horse races and trials of skill.

Never before or since have there been such idyllic days. The country was open, the grass was free; and from the pastures of Old Spain new plants were

Californian Mode of Catching Cattle, before the days of the sombrero. The vaqueros wore silk hand-kerchiefs over their heads, a custom brought from Andalusia, Spain.

(From Vischer's Pictorial of California)

SCENE AT A CALIFORNIAN RODEO.
Gathering Cattle and Separating of Stock.
(Drawing by W. H. Hilton, 1870. From Vischer's Pictorial of California)

brought in that immensely improved the range. One in particular, the *alfilería,* or filaree, provided a feed even more rich than grama. Its twisted needles becoming entangled in the wool of Spanish sheep, dropped the seed all the way from Mexico to Arizona and California. It is a grass that horses love and that sheep mow down but seldom kill; and in the fertile Coast Range valleys it sprang up like magic after the passage of the first herds.

Wild oats and foxtail and the rank-growing mustard took the place of more tender native plants and in a few years the country was transformed. It is said that the first padres as they travelled up the coast dropped mustard-seed to mark the Camino Real; and, when the golden flowers sprang up, each in the form of a cross, the Indians looked upon it as a miracle.

The Mexicans did not believe in plowing up the ground or indulging in back-breaking agriculture. Neither were they in favor of chopping down all the trees in order to build fences. Just the way God made it they left the fertile land, and so rapidly did the cattle increase that in 1805, thirty-five years after the first herd was brought in, they were killing off cattle in the San Fernando Valley because they were destroying the grass.

When, in 1849, William Manly, the scout of the lost Death Valley Party, crossed the Mojave Desert and approached San Gabriel Mission he found cattle and horses everywhere but no sign of human habitation, until in desperation he killed a yearling to keep himself from starving. It was two days before he encountered the first house—all those cattle and horses were wild.

In their movement to the north the Spaniards kept along the coast; and for fifty years they did not invade the great central valleys. There, too, the cattle and horses ran wild. If they wandered away—or were driven off by horse thieves, or the Indians, who dearly loved horse-meat—there were plenty more nearer home and nothing much to do with them. Beef was free, and the loan of a horse to any man of Spanish blood; and it was not until the trading ships opened up a market that cattle had any price.

Even then it was only two or three dollars, the value of their hides and tallow; and it is said that the whalers, with their great vats for rendering oil, were the first to think of that. Before then, hides were traded for whatever they would bring, leaving it to the sailors to drag them to the beach and put them aboard with boats. For why work when already they had everything they needed, and Indian slaves to cultivate the fields! And so satisfied were these slaves that, when freed by the Government, they asked for nothing but to go back home.

The Spanish Californians were the despair of several observers, who saw them eating boiled beans when they could have raised vegetables, neglecting to plant their wide fields to grain, and in general avoiding hard work. But the time was coming when all this would be changed—and a German butcher's boy, who lived for nothing else, would show them how to *work*. This was Henry Miller, the Cattle King, at once the greatest enemy and the best friend of the Mexicans. When he got through with them he owned most of the land they would not farm and the cattle they could not feed during the drouths. But they would have lost it, anyway, and Henry paid them cash.

When he died a few years ago he had a million head of cattle and huge ranches in three states. He began to make money on the day that he landed and kept it up all his life, and yet his method was very simple. He always bought land and he never sold any, and he made it pay from the start. When he stepped off the ship in San Francisco the story is that he walked out Market Street until he met two Mexicans coming in. They were driving three steers they had got from their father's herd and, after buying the cattle, Miller killed them by the road and hung the carcasses on a tree.

Meat was scarce, the sand-hills were swarming with newcomers, and in the course of the day Miller sold all his beef and headed back for town. But on the way he met the two brothers, who had lost all their money at monte. They were broke and dying for a drink and Henry gave them a dollar.

"Go back to your ranch," he said. "Bring me in more steers and I will pay you well for them."

37

When the Mexicans brought more cattle he gave them more money; and so on, until they were broke. Their father had lost everything and they were worse off than ever, but Miller was still their friend.

"Go back among your neighbors," he said. "Bring some of their cows and I will pay you a commission."

Then he gave them a dollar to kill their thirst and they brought in their neighbors' stock. When these men were broke he gave *them* a commission, and so on until he owned all the ranches in the neighborhood and all the cattle as well. But, no matter how broke they were, Henry would always advance them money, or give them a job handling his cattle, and the Mexicans were always his friends. He was playing the same system as a gambler who, whenever a man goes broke at his game, always gives him a dollar to eat on and says:

"Better luck next time!"

It was not Miller's fault that the Mexicans all played monte, bet on horse races, and drank at the bar. They lived for the pleasure of the moment and would borrow as long as he would lend. That is what broke the Mexican cowmen, from Oregon to the Line. They never thought how the money would be paid back but only of the pleasure it would buy.

Chapter IV

HENRY MILLER—AND THE END

THIS is the story—though it may be a fable—of how Henry Miller got his start; and from there it is very simple. He opened a slaughterhouse on the edge of San Francisco to handle the steers he bought and, when the business was going well, he went out among the Mexicans and bought more cattle—cheap. Then he hired Mexican vaqueros to drive the cows to town and they spent all their money at the games.

From San Francisco he worked south along the Santa Clara Valley until he came to the town of Gilroy, and from there he jumped the ridge into the San Joaquin Valley, where the cattle were still running wild. Here was a level plain two hundred miles long and fifty miles across, with a great river flowing down it to the sea and the grass growing high on both sides. The first ranch he bought there had the brand HH and he adopted it as his own. There were HH horses and HH cattle, and they were always better than the rest.

Being a butcher he hated the rangy Mexican cattle and bred them up with Durhams and Herefords. He brought in Morgan sires and raised a bigger breed of cow-horses—that could be used, when they got too old, to drag a scraper on the levees or do heavy work on his farms. For Miller was a man who looked far ahead, and got the most out of horses and men. He worked hard himself and expected his hands to do the same. If they didn't, he fired them and got someone else, and he was always on the run.

Rising before dawn he would climb into his buggy and with a team of fast horses drive from ranch to ranch, taking note as he went of the condition of the cattle and the fences. A thousand stories were told of his niggardly ways and a thousand more of his generosity to the poor. At Christmas he gave away tons of prime turkeys, fully dressed; and a list of his private charities would fill a book. But he was careful, and so much more thrifty than the common run of people that after three big drouths he owned everything.

When he first entered the San Joaquin Valley he marked it for his own and, no matter how much they fought him, he got possession of it and improved it. In the early days the State of California issued land script, worth about a dollar an acre and good for any Red S, or Swamp Land, not taken. Miller went into debt for millions of dollars, taking up the marshy land on both sides of the river, until he controlled over a hundred miles. Then for fifty miles he built levees to control the floods—and behind these levees he fenced in the ground and ran cattle.

It was rich soil and the sediment from the river alone was sufficient to fertilize the alfalfa; but, with so much to drain and dam and so much more to plant and irrigate, it kept him poor for years. Yet he never bought an acre that he did not improve it and put it to work growing crops; and when a drouth came, he had pasture for all his cattle—and for all the cows he could buy. That was the joker, the fable of the ant and the grasshopper, and the Mexicans who had fiddled all summer had to sing a different tune when their cattle began to die on the range. And rather than see them perish, they sold to Henry Miller who had been preparing for this for years.

The first big drouth came in 1855, and in the southern coast counties alone, over 100,000 cattle died. Another drouth came in 1863 and a million head perished in the State. Miller did his best to prevent this terrible loss and, being a butcher, he slaughtered thousands of cattle to save the hides and tallow. It was the system of the old-fashioned *matanzas*, where in carefree style the Mexicans killed their cattle for the hides; but now, instead of trading them for the silks of the Indies, they found themselves miserably poor.

They had mortgages on their property, but Miller borrowed the money and bought it, until hardly a Mexican Grant was left. Then he turned around and stocked the depleted range with better cattle, which could stand the drouth. The price of meat went up and Miller took the profit, so that it was said that after the drouth of 1888 he made eight million dollars in five years. The same dry years that were poison to the Mexicans were money in the bank for Henry;

yet he had shown them twice before what to do in case of a drouth, only the Mexicans would not do it. If, after it was over, Henry Miller owned most of the land and cattle, he had saved the State from irreparable losses, for without him conditions would have been worse.

He had no monopoly on his system, which was always to buy land and never to sell it, and never to sell a cow with his brand on it. He got rid of the scrubby Mexican stock and substituted Durhams and Herefords, and the Henry Miller horses were the pride of the countryside, wherever cowboys worked cattle. One of his old-time cowhands was Len Myers, whom I met on the Sespe range in 1902. His *tapaderos* were so long they almost reached the ground—his horse stepped on them when he ran along a hillside—but it was one of the prettiest horses I ever saw, and could turn around on a dime.

Len told me some good stories about Henry Miller and the surprising things Miller would do when he came by to inspect the range. Every boss was on his toes, for he noted every gate that sagged, every sorebacked horse, every hog that was overfed or underfed. If his cattle were lying asleep in the shade and a man came along the ditch and woke them up, Henry would fire him and make a little talk.

"Walk in the sun," he would say. "Don't make them cows get up. Leave 'em alone—they're making fat."

Another man hung a hide on the fence to dry and Henry fired *him*. He had hung it with the hair side out.

"Lend me your knife," he said to a ranch hand; and then he fired him.

"I won't have a man working for me," he said, "that hasn't got a knife."

When the hobos stopped at a Henry Miller ranch-house he fed them and kept them overnight. Then they had to move on—to the next ranch-house. He fed them to gain their good will and to keep some vengeful vagrant from setting fire to his haystacks; and he gave them a bunk for the same reason, to keep them from sleeping in the hay and setting it afire with cigarettes. It is said that for one day he took the advice of hundreds of his friends and turned every hobo away. Then, cursing them for busybodies, he rescinded the order; for the whole length of the San Joaquin Valley was lit up with fires from the haystacks they had lit.

He drove up to a ranch-house one day, just in time to see the Chinese cook burst out of the kitchen with a bread knife in his hand. A man had sneaked in and stolen a pie and, as the Chinaman ran after him, the ranch hand circled around the bole of a big cottonwood. Then while the Chink kept after him, his pigtail flying, the white man caught up from behind and jerked him over backwards. It was all very mysterious and terrifying to the cook and, when he saw the Boss looking on, he went in and packed up his things. He knew he was fired, but Henry Miller stopped him.

"No," he said. "You good man—you go back there. And the next so-and-so you ketch stealing your pies, you kill him."

Then he gave strict orders for all ranch hands to stay out of the kitchen and leave the Chink alone. He was doing his duty and protecting the company property, and he kept him for many years.

About 1910 I was trapping in the mountains back of San Ardo at a place called Bitter Water when I met another man with Henry Miller stories to tell. It was Gib Davis, who lived on a ranch a few miles away, and Henry Miller in riding through had seen a drawing made by his sister and given the girl ten dollars for it. It was true frontier art, with big-horned cows jumping impossible gulches as they fled and a very flossy-looking cowboy riding after them and whirling a Mother Hubbard loop.

Some people would not have called it art at all, as the little girl was self-taught, but the Davises were one happy family and nothing was too good to be said of Henry Miller. His headquarters ranch was only a few miles north, up at Gilroy, and when he came back he was going to buy another picture which the young lady artist was drawing for him.

With his cattle ranging over a thousand hills Miller was more or less at the mercy of a host of little ranchers, mostly Mexicans. They could kill a lot of

44

cows, and did, but Henry had the same talk for all.

"When your wife and children are hungry and you are out of beef, kill a cow, but kill an old one. Then hang the hide on the fence, so I can see you are on the square."

Henry was always dropping in on them unexpectedly and, no matter how many cows they had skinned, that was all right if the hides were on the fence. And, instead of killing yearlings as nesters generally do, the Mexicans were careful to rope out some old cow, and to jerk the rest of the meat to dry. Every time they found cattle bogged down in the quicksand they dropped everything and pulled them out and, all in all, they saved more cows than they killed.

No matter how rank the cow-stealing got, Henry Miller would almost never prosecute. If they demanded a jury trial they would come free anyway, and he wanted the people to be his friends. He needed friends, for a man cannot come into the country the way he did, start at San Francisco and move south, practically taking over the range, without making a lot of enemies.

One day he was driving through Pacheco Pass from Gilroy to the San Joaquin Valley when he was held up and robbed by a couple of Mexicans, who belonged to a cattle-rustling gang. He knew in a general way who they were and where they came from and, as he always paid his bills with HH drafts, they did not get over twenty dollars in cash. But he needed some

change to pay his way across the ferry and when they
waved him on he said:

"Boys, I need a couple of dollars to travel on and if
you'll lend me the money I'll pay you back the first
time I see you."

The Mexicans laughed and handed over the money
and, a year or two later, when he was driving into
Gilroy, he met them, riding out.

"Hey! Wait a minute!" he hollered and, in spite of
all their protestations, he insisted upon giving them
the money.

He liked the Mexican people and their lighthearted
way of doing things and, though he and others like
him had gotten possession of nearly all of their
ranches, he always hired them as horse-breakers and
round-up hands. He knew how to laugh and how to
take a joke; and so, till he died, they loved him. If
they had failed in their struggle for financial inde-
pendence they still retained their old-world politeness
and the hospitable ways of their kind.

Long after the Mexicans had lost out in California
I met in Arizona a man who still lived as if the world
had not changed. He was J. L. Hubbell, son of a Captain in the United States Army and a Spanish lady
from Santa Fe; and at his trading post at Ganado on
the Navajo Reservation he was at all times the Spanish
gentleman. As in the days before the Gringos came he
had his feudal retainers, thousands of Indians who

called him Don Lorenzo and many Mexican servants who had remained in his family all their lives.

His great adobe house was open to all who came, and he told me that only once in forty years had he turned a man away from his door. That was when an Englishman, after being told that he was welcome and to be sure and stay longer the next time, had left two dollars on the bureau of his room, in payment for what he had received. That night in a terrible storm there was a knock at the door. It was the Englishman, who had been turned back by a devastating flood, but J. L. Hubbell closed his door.

"No," he said. "You have insulted me, sir, by daring to offer to pay me."

He drove him out into the storm and that was the last of him.

But to everybody else he was the kind and gracious host, and in no way could you get even with him. If you admired some beautiful blanket he would insist upon giving it to you; and when, to get revenge, you tried to buy another one at his Post, his servants would pass the word along and he would tell the clerk to sell it at cost. Or below cost. There was an amiable conspiracy to keep you from paying anything; and when he gave his Chicken Pull, a great fiesta for all the Indians, he carried it off like a king.

No Spanish Don in the days of old could conduct things in such lordly style. At a great double table

47

at least forty feet long he served dinner to his guests in relays. Every room was filled with his friends and, on rich piles of blankets, he bedded down the rest in the hay. Deputations of Navajos entered his office all day to talk with Venerable Respected Mexican; and, while some brought gifts to him, he was giving out more gifts, until it seemed he would impoverish himself.

Every morning, on the plain before the Post, there were horse races and wrestling matches, and naked Indians swinging down from their ponies to snatch buried roosters by their heads. There was singing and dancing until far into the night; and when it was all over, after four days of festivities, Don Lorenzo bade us all farewell, telling us to be sure to come sooner and stay longer next time.

When at last he got into financial difficulties he was saved by his loyal son, who sold his two best trading posts to relieve his father of debt. Then young Lorenzo moved to the Hopi Reservation, where he began all over again. But he was still the proud Spanish gentleman, having learned nothing and forgotten nothing, as far as hospitality is concerned; for to this day if you stop at Don Lorenzo's trading post you are welcome and everything is free. He is sincerely offended if you try to pay for anything, not realizing that in this day and age he is probably the only man left in the West to whom hospitality is a religion.

The last time I saw his father, the Venerable Respected Mexican, I spoke of the free-handed way in which his house was run and he told me this story on his new mayordomo, or steward.

"At the end of the first month he came to me and said:

" 'Don Lorenzo, do you realize how many meals you have given away?'

" 'Why, no,' I said. 'How many?'

" 'Three thousand, four hundred and forty-two, sir!'

" 'Well, Manuel,' I said, 'you are a new man and that is very well for the first month. Next month try to give away six thousand, eight hundred and eighty-four.' "

That was the old Spanish *caballero*, still living in the past, thinking nothing of money and everything of friends—his religion, hospitality. But these ways cannot last much longer. The Mexican people are not geared up to meet the tempo of this barbed-wire and gasoline age. They have learned to live on little and to keep off the rushing highways—back in the side canyons, where it is more like the old days and vaqueros can still ride the trails. Yet, once every year, when Fiesta Day comes, they troop into Santa Barbara or Salinas or Livermore and find themselves neither despised nor poor.

They get out their old finery and the girls look very pretty in black lace and yellow silk, with high-backed Spanish combs in their hair. The American

girls try to look like them, but behind the old costumes there is a way of wearing them which cannot
be learned in a day. The young men sit their horses
in a way that we lack and, while the Americans own
most of the silver-mounted saddles, the Mexican cowboys ride best.

So gorgeous are the costumes at these Rodeos and
Fiesta Days that a new style in riding has been set.
An English saddle looks awkward and unsuited to the
country, and in the last ten years a sudden change
has taken place. You would be barred from the Fiesta
Procession now if you appeared with a bowler hat.
There is no costume like the Spanish, and in ten years
more the Eastern styles will be forgotten.

After their long period of oblivion the Mexican
people have come back to their own; and we have to
concede that, both in art and horsemanship, we have
much to learn from them. It has been bred in their
bones for thousands of years; and a man on a horse
is still a *caballero,* no matter whether he is rich or
poor.

Len Myers.

An old-time Henry Miller cowboy, on one of the Morgan-bred HH horses.

(Photograph by Dane Coolidge, 1902)

TWO: COWBOYS IN ARIZONA

PANCHO VILLA.

Sitting on the throne of President Diaz, but for him it is an empty honor.
Zapata and his bandits had beat him to the City of Mexico and robbed
the big saddle store.

(Rose Collection)

Chapter V

VAQUEROS

THE best riders and ropers in the world! Charley Russell, the Western artist, said he had never seen cowboys until he stopped off at Chihuahua City, Mexico, and saw a bunch of Terrazas' vaqueros putting on a show in the square. They would ride straight at a stone wall and, when it seemed certain that both horse and man would be killed, they would turn and avoid death by a hair. With their rawhide *reatas* they could catch any foot of any horse as he passed—and all on the dead run—just for fun!

Terrazas had thousands of them working for him, for he owned half the state of Chihuahua and hundreds of thousands of cattle. They were peons, but they were happy, because they were riding good horses—and without a horse a Mexican is nothing. But when Pancho Villa came down out of the mountains and started his revolution he gave them another idea—to *own* these fine horses that they were riding for their masters.

When he began his triumphant march on the City of Mexico, all his *muchachos* could think about was the big store on the Avenida Cinco de Mayo where they carried the finest saddles in the world—and theirs for the taking. But another bandit, Emiliano Zapata, beat them to it. He was operating around Cuernavaca, just over the mountains, and when the Villistas rode in, there wasn't a saddle left.

Of course there was the National Treasury to loot, and the jewelry stores, and the Monte de Piedad. But to a Mexican nothing is quite so grand as a cactus-tree saddle, its horn as broad on top as a soup plate and gleaming with polished silver, a tiger-skin *sobre jalma* thrown over the back, inlaid spurs weighing a pound apiece and on his head a silver-white sombrero with gold hawk-bells hanging down behind.

That was worth dying for, and gladly they would have died, but the bandits from Guerrero had stolen every saddle in the store. Villa had his picture taken in the Presidential Chair—with Zapata looking very sulky over being given second place. But, although Villa had sat on the throne of Porfirio Diaz, it was a hollow victory for him and soon he was back in Chihuahua.

There he took possession of the golden horses of Terrazas—sent to Mexico by Queen Isabella and for centuries never bought or sold—and boarded the train for Nogales, Arizona, to make a lasting peace with Obregon. He rode down the main street on Rayo del Sol, one of the most beautiful *palomillos* in the world, and his Dorados followed behind him on the pick of all the horses in Mexico.

A glorious sight—it would have made a fine picture—but the Yaqui Indians spoiled everything. They promised to shoot Pancho on sight if he set foot on the soil of Sonora, so he waited until the dusk put a blur on their sights before he made his dash. Then he galloped back, having shown them he would not take a dare, and the next day he was headed for Chihuahua.

It was in September, 1914, and the whole world was at war. The Germans had invaded Belgium and were marching on Paris; while just across the Line 2200 Yaquis were holding Nogales, Sonora. The big question was: did they come *bueno* or *malo?* Were they out for peace or war? They had stood off Pancho Villa and sent him on his way, but those who had cattle in Sonora were bringing them across the Line. Theoretically, the Yaquis were supporting Governor Maytorena, who in turn was supporting Carranza; but within the month they were fighting again. It was like that all the time.

Meanwhile a lot of cattle had been brought into Arizona, and further to the west in the Baboquivari Valley an old-time rodeo was coming off. It was the last big Mexican round-up in Arizona, and I spent two months getting the photographs. The next year the round-up was taken over by Texans and, a drouth setting in, most of the cattle died or were driven out of the country.

Chapter VI

BABOQUIVARI

IT IS a beautiful country—though a desert, of course. A broad valley between cathedral-domed mountains, extending from Tucson to Sásabe, on the Mexican Line. But while the revolution was going on the Mexican soldiers were eating a lot of beef; and before they got through with it there was hardly a cow left, except a few up in the hills. The grassy plains of Sonora became like the prairies of the Middle West before the white men came, a sea of waving grama; and, for lack of beef, the armies had to disband. That's what stopped the revolutions.

But in 1914 the cattle-buyers were shipping them out by the thousand; and the Mexican owners, rather than suffer a total loss, were shoving them across the Line. Down the deep storm-ditch which ran through Nogales, Arizona, the gaunt "adobe" cattle were pouring in like a flood, wild and fighty, just off the range. And, through the customhouse at Sásabe, other thousands had been brought in and spread out over the Valley.

There was an import duty of about three dollars a head; and, seeing their country being stripped of cattle, the Mexicans hung on an export duty of ten dollars more. It was to beat this that small herds were brought up at night and drifted across the Line; and

Mexican vaqueros in the Baboquivari Valley, dragging out a steer for beef. But before they kill him they want to play with him awhile. They are always roping at something.

(Photograph by Dane Coolidge)

Down the deep storm-ditch which ran through Nogales, Arizona, the gaunt "adobe" cattle were pouring in like a flood. The Mexican owners smelled war.

(Photograph by Dane Coolidge)

the customs guards were kept busy, rounding them up on the American side.

But the grass was fine, there was water in the often dry lake; and for the last time—though they did not know it yet—the Mexicans rode in for the rodeo. Arivaca was headquarters for all that desert country, an old Mexican town nearly wiped out time and again by the Apaches, but dozing calmly on. I put up at the hotel—kept by Carmen Zepeda, a cousin of my old friend Johnny Jones—but got in wrong at the start with her only other boarder. He was a foreigner of forbidding mien—later arrested as a German spy— and he absolutely refused to speak to me.

Not knowing his nationality, I had repeated a story then going the rounds at Nogales, about an expedition the Smithsonian was sending out. The German drive into France had been stopped with great loss and this expedition was to get two Germans, one male and one female. The implication was obvious—that in a few short months there would be no Germans left; and to the poor spy, cut off from his fatherland, the jest must have come as a cruel blow.

I was out of luck all around, my letters of introduction not bringing even a pleasant look, but I was saved from the company of this German by a carefree young cattle inspector named Wooddell. He had a roach-maned blue horse of which he was very proud, and when he found out that I was a horse-photographer, he invited me out to the ranch. This did not belong to him but to the Arivaca Cattle Company, at whose headquarters he was a guest; but Nonie Bernard, the Superintendent, was just as friendly with his welcome and, after the Western way, I moved in.

I had just sworn an oath never to impose myself on strangers or horn in when I was not wanted; but here—without any letters—I found myself a welcome guest. In the absence of his wife, Nonie was keeping bachelor's hall, with a Mexican girl coming in to cook for him, and Leslie Wooddell for company. Besides these he had as next-door neighbors Ramon Ahumada and his wife, and there was not one in the country more hospitable and good-hearted than Ramon.

He had been foreman for the Company when Nonie was a boy and his father a cattle king, and now he was part owner in the Company. Coming up into Arizona from Sonora he had distinguished himself as a horse-tamer—a man who could lay his hand on many a wild bronk that nobody else could touch. He was a master of men, too, and the mentor of more than one young Eastern boy who had come West to learn the cattle business.

In a fine house of his own, furnished in exquisite taste, he lived with the most loving wife that I have ever seen. When she ate at the table she often sat on his knee while he fed her like a bird—a beautiful Spanish woman of good family. Yet it was said that Ramon was pure Yaqui. But whatever his ancestry,

he was born a gentleman and the tales of his generosity were almost fabulous. Like most Mexicans he had
a *compadre*—any man who has been christened by
the same godfather, or one to whom he is greatly at-
tached. It is a sort of Damon and Pythias relationship,
like the American "pardners," and Ramon was so de-
voted to Gabriel Angula that anything which Gabe
admired he gave to him. To try him, Angula sometimes praised his saddle and bridle and without a word
Ramon would strip them off and put them on his
horse. It was the talk of the countryside, where *compadres* were common, but none like Gabe and Ramon.

As for Angula, he was a cattle-buyer and horse-
trader, a man of very irregular features and a rather
macabre cast of countenance. There were those who
said he took advantage of Ramon and, while I was
taking Ahumada's picture, I witnessed the crowning
test of their friendship. Ramon was the owner of
Moro, the best cow-horse in Arivaca, and the fastest
racer in the country. He was a Steeldust stallion, with
a silky white coat and the black flaring nostrils of his
breed; and, to pretty him up for his picture, Ramon
had got out his silver-mounted bridle and martingale.

But in the middle of our picture-making Angula
rode up and looked on with a wry, amused smile.

"That is a very fine bridle you have," he said; and
Ramon took it off his horse.

"It is yours," he answered. "And this martingale goes with it. No! I insist! It is yours!"

They traded, right there, but Angula was not satisfied. Or perhaps he was still trying out his *compadre,* to see how far he could go. The silverwork was very beautiful, but it had been made right there in town and the bit-maker could hammer out more.

"No!" he exclaimed, when the rigging had been changed, "it does not look well on my horse. Take it back, *compadre,* and put it on Moro. He is the finest horse in the country."

Ramon stepped down and uncinched his saddle.

"You are right," he said, still smiling. "It looks better on him. He is yours."

Then, despite all protests, he changed saddles with Angula and rode off on the bay horse. And, to make the trade complete, he exchanged hats with Gabe and put on his old blue jumper.

The country was in a furore when Angula rode Moro into town with Ramon's superb martingale and bridle; but the people were slow to believe that Ahumada had given away his horse. For Moro was so perfectly trained that on the cutting-ground he was king, and, if his master had not declined to run any more races, he would have won all the money in the country. But when Ramon acknowledged that the gift had been made, the word was passed around that he had got tired of racing horses and his wife had begged him to quit.

RAMON ON MORO.

His Steeldust stallion, the best running-horse in the country. But when Angula, his *compadre*, praised the horse, Ramon said: "He is yours."

(Photograph by Dane Coolidge)

Despite all protests Ramon changed saddles with Angula and rode off on the bay horse. And, to make the trade complete, he exchanged hats with Gabe and put on his old blue jumper.

(Photograph by Dane Coolidge)

What was behind it all, or how it came out, I never fully knew, for with the rodeo coming on I had to drop everything and try to get *me* a horse. That was possible, of course—but how to get a saddle when every man was riding was something else again. But it was easy for Leslie Wooddell, who had a way of getting things, and he appeared with the best horse I ever rode, with saddle and bridle complete.

After a miracle like that I did not question him too closely at the time, but before I left the country I discovered that it was the fortunes of war which had put Chula in my hands. He was the private mount of a rich Sonora cattleman, who had left him with Ramon Ahumada to keep the Mexican soldiers from stealing him. And, since a photographer with a nine-pound camera slung on his saddle would not be riding very fast or far, the ever-generous Ramon had passed him on to me. He was perfectly gentle, but fast and easy-gaited, and I was sometimes tempted to leave my camera behind just to gallop off across the plains.

My friend Leslie Wooddell was a great character in the country, being known far and wide as Cabezon on account of his big head. He had been a cattle inspector for several years and ridden far out across the Papago Desert, where a white man was far from welcome. Among the Pimas he was called Montezuma because, like that mythical personage, he made fire with flint and steel. For the same reason the Papagos called him Sonora, since the Sonora Mexicans used flints; but around Arivaca he was Cabezon.

He could speak Spanish as well as English, knew a lot of the Papago words, and had qualified for his job as assistant cattle inspector by buying mules and horses from the Pimas. He knew Indian signs, also, and most of the dim trails that led out through their land, for both tribes made a business of picking up stray cattle; and any cow that crossed the Baboquivari Mountains was sure to lose her calf—and likely to turn into jerked beef.

The top of the mountains was the dead-line, and the Indian agents rather justified their wards in running off the strays. Otherwise the white men would move in and take over all the range. The Papagos had built up quite a traffic in stolen cows, bringing cattle from below the Line up the narrow canyon to the Baboquivari, where they traded them to the ranchers for strays from further east and maybe ran off a few to take home. The king of all that country for many years had been Colonel Sturgis of La Osa, and they never stole from him, but the rest of the Americans had to watch their cattle or they would find them growing less and less.

There were four or five big cattle companies, all controlled by Americans; but that was as far as it went. The round-up and the country was in the hands of old-time Mexicans, and likely to stay so for some time. But when a drouth came on and the lake in the sink went dry the Americans had bored some very deep wells and so gained control of the range. The best well of all was on the flat at Buenos Aires, where the La Osa Company had its corrals and it was there that the rodeo began.

Chapter VII

THE RODEO AT BUENOS AIRES

CABEZON and I rode down the long wash from Arivaca past Punta de Agua, where the water stopped; and as we ambled along, another officer joined us—John Glissan, United States Customs Inspector. John was tall and lanky, with a drooping moustache, and he was as proud of his lemon-colored pack mule, Limón, as Leslie was of Blue. Limón came rambling along behind with Glissan's bed lashed on his back and not even a halter on his neck, and with true mule perversity he would stop along the road, even turn back.

"I'll bet you a dollar," offered John, "that he ketches up in ten minutes."

But as Wooddell shrugged a shoulder I declined to take him up. It was just as well for me, for at some mysterious sign from his master, the mule came galloping up.

"That's the finest mule in this country," declared Glissan. "I wouldn't take two hundred dollars for him. And any time I'd sell him old Limón would be right back. He's crazy about this horse."

That is a common weakness with mules, and John had some good stories to tell, but most of his anecdotes were in the Cousin Jack lingo which he had learned while working in the mines. But a Cornish fortune-

CABEZON WOODDELL.

The American cattle inspector, waiting for the herd to come in. Among the Pima Indians he was called Montezuma, because he made fire with flint and steel.

(*Photograph by Dane Coolidge*)

The U. S. Customs Inspector and his lemon-colored pack mule, Limon. John was very proud of Limon, and no matter how far he lagged behind, was always ready to bet he'd be back.

(Photograph by Dane Coolidge)

teller, gazing into a cup of tea, had changed the course
of his life. She had told him he would die underground, as most miners more or less expect, and he
had fooled her by quitting his job and getting another
one riding the Line. Not in twenty years had he gone
underground, but when the main street of Tombstone
caved in, taking a delivery wagon into the depths, it
had given him a bad scare.

Now he kept away from mining towns altogether
and was content to ride the border, getting a mild
excitement from running down smugglers and putting Mexican cattle across the Line. As we rode down
into the Valley, which was dotted with fat cows, a
couple of Mexicans approached and Cabezon turned
out to question them.

"Now you see?" observed John. "He's a galvanized
Mex. They ain't a white man in this country that
won't ride off and leave you to trade cigarettes with
some Mexican."

But Leslie knew his men and after the customary
salutations, and shaking hands, he unhooked in fluent
Spanish.

"Did you see three Americans going by?" he asked,
and the Mexicans set him right.

"No," they said. "One American and two Tex-
anos."

"Now who the hell," said Wooddell, "is that other
Teehanno? Ronstadt has had one running his outfit
all summer, but he's the only Texan in the country."

We had heard about the first of these outlanders, whom the Mexicans truly believe belong to another race of men. The first thing he had done was fire both the vaqueros and do the work of three men himself. Everything he did was different, and he couldn't speak a word of Spanish. He had put out salt, gentling the Ronstadt cows and encouraging them to water at the home tank—and he never swung a rope! It was a strange way for a cowboy to handle cattle, but now the owner of the La Osa outfit had sent back to Texas for another one.

He was waiting at the corrals when we got to Buenos Aires, and if ever there was a lonely Texan it was Red. He had been out eight days with about twenty vaqueros, and not a word of English! No one to talk to; and the Mexicans polite, but distant. They knew who he was and why he had been sent for—to look over the range, get the run of the country and then, perhaps, fire *them*.

Roman Azebeda, their easy-going mayordomo, or round-up boss, had been running the rodeo for years. He worked the cattle the way his people had always worked them, and the vaqueros were behind him to a man. It is no use arguing with a Mexican that it is wrong to rope a cow. The Mexicans had always roped them, and the fact that the price of fat steers had gone up had nothing to do with the case. Not with the Mexicans, anyway; but with the owner it was different.

66

The Rodeo at Buenos Aires

A new school of cowmen had sprung up, along with the price of beef, and they figured that when a cow-brute is roped and busted he is damaged at least ten dollars' worth the minute he hits the ground. He loses weight, his hair turns the wrong way, he gets rough and off his feed; and when the cattle-buyer sees him he cuts him out of the herd. When a cow and her calf were worth twenty-five dollars it didn't make so much difference, but now that they were selling up to seventy, even the Texans took notice. Not the old-time Texans, who expected to lose a few cows anyway; but such modern, up-to-date cowmen as Colonel Goodnight who had been studying these things out.

The owner of the La Osa outfit, being a keen American business man, was much given to this mode of thought. He knew that there was a better way of handling cattle, without all this riding and roping. And when Ronstadt's Texan did the work of three men without letting down his throw-rope, Mr. Coberly sent back and got Texas Red. "Colorado," the Mexicans called him, and when he saw us coming he nearly wept for joy.

According to Tex there wasn't a Mexican in the outfit that knew the first thing about cattle. All they thought about was shaking out a ten-foot loop and roping at everything that moved. And when they brought in the herd every rascal followed along behind, beating the drag over the tail with his rope.

67

Now back in Texas. . . . We camped at Buenos Aires and listened to Red talk cow, for that was all he knew, and it was easy to see he would never be very popular with the Mexicans.

Not only did he have a different idea of the cow business—he was the point, the extreme tip, of that wave of Texas cowmen which was moving west like a wall. The cattle ranges of Texas were rapidly being fenced in and the cowboys were on the move. In 1904 a Texan had been a rarity in Arizona. Now, ten years later, they had taken half the State and were looking over the rest. They came with money, too—the price of their herds back home—and always with a pistol in their belt.

That gun was not necessary, but they kept it in sight as a notice to all Mexicans that they would do well to give the Texan the road. Otherwise he was liable to get ranicky and put some *paisano* in his place. The Mexicans had sensed this the first day, but as Roman was still in charge of the rodeo he ran it in true Mexican style. To these carefree individuals it was a big social and sporting event, a kind of fiesta and roping contest combined; while to the Texans it was a business proposition, the object being to brand as many calves as possible and cut out cattle to ship.

Being run in true Mexican fashion, the La Osa round-up was, of course, a day late. Some of the vaqueros had gone to another ranch by mistake; but Madre, the cook, had arrived with the chuck-wagon

RYE MILES.

Livestock Inspector, formerly sergeant in the Arizona Rangers. The high-crowned hat, apron shaps, short grass-rope, *and* the pistol mark this man for a straight Texan.

(*Photograph by Dane Coolidge*)

"Madre", or Mother, cooked for seventy cowboys and carried their scanty bed-rolls on his chuck-wagon. Every time a beef was killed he "jerked" the extra meat and hung it out to dry.

(*Photograph by Dane Coolidge*)

and we all had plenty to eat. Every ranch in the country had sent in a stray-man—and those who were not so fortunate as to get a job drifted in to work for nothing. Believe it or not, there were seventy Mexicans on this rodeo; and Madre kept his fires burning late, cooking oil cans full of beans to feed them.

We slept on the hard ground in two camps—the Mexicans rolled up in a single, chicken-skin blanket, the Americans with a horse-load of bedding apiece. There was Rye Miles, the County livestock inspector, whom I had known as a sergeant in the Rangers; and Cabezon, his deputy, who could draw brands in the dust all day. There was another Arizona Ranger on his way to round up some cow thieves, the Customs Inspector, two Texas cowboys, and myself.

Four officers, two cowboys, and a picture-man—it showed how much we belonged. We sat out under the stars, telling stories in competition; and the Mexicans, having eaten their fill, began to sing. First one would start off in a high falsetto, another would join in on the alto, a third would come in on the bass, and they would all end up in a long minor chord, sustained till they ran out of breath. It was "The Twenty-fourth of May," a ballad of the last round-up, with a verse for every man who had been there, and I thought it was wonderful, but nobody else stopped to listen. Then Red Tex, the man who was to be the next superintendent—perhaps—spit over his shoulder and spoke.

"Listen to them damned Mexicans," he said.

"They're just like a bunch of kyotes. As soon as they get their bellies full they all begin to sing."

The Mexicans were more polite—they are naturally polite—but if they had expressed their opinion of Red it would have been equally unflattering. And, while they all professed not to understand a word of English, it was perfectly evident that they had caught the general drift of his remarks. Cabezon went over and exchanged a few remarks with them before they went to bed, but the singing had ceased abruptly and Red was off to a very bad start.

In the morning, although the cook was feeding twenty vaqueros, Roman decided he did not have enough hands to make a proper drive. So, following the orders of his thrifty American boss not to waste any good beef, he combed the range for the oldest cow he could find. By the rings on her horns she was fourteen years of age, but that night we had fresh meat.

Meanwhile the Mexicans spent the day in the primitive occupations of their kind. A pair of *compadres* got out a sack of horsehair, jerked from the tail of many a horse, and squatted down in the corner to twist and plait a hair-rope. Another pair took the hide of the oldest cow and pegged it out to dry, preparatory to making a rawhide *reata*. The rest gathered about the beef and cut off slices to broil, while for sport they rode three bronco horses and put on a couple of races. That night Roman spread his slicker on the ground, stuck a candle on it and opened up a monte game that lasted the full two months. He and his banker started off with eight dollars and after they had been playing about a month Red Tex sauntered by, matched the stake and busted the bank the first deal.

A dime at a time they had built it up from eight dollars to twenty-two and then this red-headed Texan had cleaned them and passed on, laughing. He was one of the luckiest gamblers in the world and at craps could throw a natural any time. We Americans had learned not to play with him—and after that he was barred from the monte game—but it did not add to the *entente cordiale* to have him win Roman's whole pot. But it is one of the rules of the game that players can bet on either the top or bottom layout up to the limit of the bank, and the first "gate" that was shown Red won.

The next morning, while every star was blazing in the sky, there was a distant yell from the horse-rustlers, a thunder of approaching hoofs, and the *remuda* came in out of the darkness and poured into the round corral. Then the cook beat on his dish-pan, and by the flickering light of his fire, we grabbed plates and cups and "tools" and ate enough to last all day. There was no hearty meal at midday as with most well-ordered Texas outfits, and on the other hand no fast from morning till night as with the hard-riding Arizona cowboys. After breakfast each man took a dutch-oven biscuit and four or five cubes of loaf sugar for a "loncha," and that had to last all day.

At the first gleam of dawn they went out to catch up their horses and there was a rush that jarred the heavy posts as the first Mexican roped his mount. Half a hundred watchful heads rose above the cloud of dust as he led his horse towards the gate and then, in a circle of milling horses and flying *reatas,* the yelling Mexicans made their casts. It was a scene of the wildest excitement, the Mexicans were fairly drunk with joy; but the two Texans, roosting like vultures on the fence, looked on with glum disapproval.

"What? Swing a rope in a corral?" yapped Red. "Chowse your horses around like that? W'y, back in Texas—"

It seemed the Texans had discovered, after all these years, that it is bad for horses to chase them around through the dust; and to whirl a Mother Hubbard loop in the horse-pen is barred with any Texas outfit. But the great day had come when the rodeo was to begin and the Mexicans took a chance on getting trampled to death in order to be up and away. They rode off skylarking, the air full of flying *reatas* as they roped each other's horses by the tail. Some bronks clamped down on the *reatas* and bucked all over the flat, friends rode in to help their laughing comrades, and foes gave whoops of joy. It was a gala day, a fiesta, not a sordid workaday round-up, and when the fireworks were over Roman and his vaqueros rode out to comb the eastern hills.

As their fathers had done before them they had separated into two bands to form the wings of a circle, and all along the way the *caporal* would drop off men until the great ring was complete. Then Roman held up his hat and brought it down towards the ground, the hills echoed to shrill yells, and the vaqueros started the drive. All was done by rote, as it had been for many years, and the wise old range cows, seeing once more the circling horsemen, turned instinctively to the distant *parada*-ground where they knew they would be safe from pursuit.

All the Americans, even Red, passed up the long ride over rocky ridges and headed for the hold-up grounds, nine miles away to the southeast. It was hot, and why ride down a good horse when the Mexicans were so crazy to go? We dismounted on the slope of a distant hill and looked off down into Mexico, and if the Texans had their way we would never stop until all that good cow-country was ours. It seemed as if destiny was driving us on and, before the fighting ended, we would take all Mexico as our fathers had taken the Far West.

The Texans stood silent, sweeping the vast stretch before them with restless, sun-squinched eyes, and the one Mexican who was with us kept discreetly in the rear as if knowing he was not wanted. A moving speck

73

showed dimly in the notch of the pass, then three or four behind him, raking the country along the Line. A horseman loomed big against the skyline to the east, waving his broad-brimmed hat, and on the wind we could hear the musical calls of the vaqueros as they pushed their cattle down.

"Hooch! Hooch! Hooch! Who-hah! Who-hah!"

From the canyon above us there came a rush, a clatter of hoofs, and a bunch of wild, mountain cattle charged out across the flat. This was the signal for the watchful Americans, who were there to help hold up the herd, and they mounted and dashed away. Cows were coming from everywhere, puffing and bellowing, tossing their heads, skating over the rocks as each dash for freedom was checked, then turning and ramping on.

The Mexican vaqueros, their horses blown and gaunted, pressed in to form a great circle and see what they had caught. But there was no changing of mounts, no scouting around for a drink of water. While the cows were finding their calves, a fire was lit, the branding irons were put over it and Roman rode into the herd. Threading slowly through the mass he noted the mother of every calf, then shook out his rope and threw.

There was a swish as the slender rawhide *reata* cut through the air and the loop fell over the calf's head. The trained horse turned instantly and set out for the fire at a trot. It was the first calf of the rodeo and a dozen eager boys rushed out to pull it down. Several clutched at his rope, others grappled with the calf. They fought not only with the calf but each other, and when it went down, it was covered with Mexicans.

A vaquero ran out with a hot running-iron and burned a huge brand on its hip, others competed in marking its ears. It was the first calf of the 1914 rodeo! But, in a little group by themselves, the Americans looked on and smiled scornfully, while Red told how they branded in Texas. At roping and dragging out calves, however, the Texans did well not to compete, for the Mexicans were better at the game.

"Why shouldn't they be?" complained Red. "They're roping all the time!"

And so, indeed, they were. When there was nothing else to rope at the Mexicans would work on each other. They could catch each other's horses by the tail, a feat which calls for a lightning-like precision and produces some startling results. "Heel-flies," grim old Rye Miles called them, and they were always at the heels of some cow. If there was no other way of starting a little excitement they would let some wild one escape from the herd, then ride whooping to haze her back.

Three black and silent Papagos came galloping up and stopped short to look around. Then they recognized Cabezon, who had been out through their country, and rode over to shake hands.

"Talk about your roping and riding," observed

Cabezon, after the Indians had ridden away, "you ought to be over at San Miguel when the Papagos have their roder. They come down out of those mountains from every direction, like crows that have sighted a dead horse, and all you can see is their dust. They've got a big corral built around the only water in the country, and they trap their cattle and horses when they come in at night for a drink.

"The next morning the Indians come in from everywhere, ride up to within fifty yards and stop. Never say hello or nothing—just take down their rope and fly at it. These Mexicans are bad enough, but I've seen *twen-ty-one* ropes on one cow, and more of them in the air. The Papagos ride their horses at a gallop and drive their cattle at a gallop—always. No, believe me, these *paisanos* are tame."

The Papagos had come over to claim their strays, for they knew their legal rights; but according to the white men, and especially the Arizona Ranger, they never gave up a stray. As for visiting Americans and Mexicans, they were received with a surly distrust which strongly resembled hate. Even the officers of the law kept out of their country unless in pursuit of fugitives; and for two hundred miles, from Baboquivari Peak to the Gulf of California, the Papagos ruled the land.

A vaquero mounted on a *bayo* or buckskin horse, one of the sturdiest breeds in the West.

(Photograph by Dane Coolidge)

ROMAN ACEBEDA.

The La Osa *mayordomo*, pointing to the far ride up which his cowboy must ride.

(Photograph by Dane Coolidge)

Chapter VIII

CUTTING THE HERD

RED TEX sat silent as the branding went on, watching the Mexicans from under his big hat; but when the cutting began Roman rode up and invited him into the herd. It was very graciously done—by signs, of course—for Roman was a perfect gentleman, and Red showed them what he could do. His horse was fresh, while the Mexicans' were fagged; but on top of all that, Red knew how. While the Mexicans, in pairs, were racing to and fro, trying to cut out certain cows from the herd, Red rode in slowly, looking over the strange brands until at last he picked out a cow.

He rode after her quietly, following her as she turned, and at the second touch of the reins his trained cutting-horse spotted her. After that it was hard to say which of the two was in command, so perfectly did they work together, and the cow and her calf were walked to the edge of the herd. Then the cow turned back, but the horse beat her to it; she dodged and turned again, but he was there; she dashed down the line and Red outran her and cut her off from the herd. She stopped to think it over, and as Red ambled towards her she gave up and trotted away.

That was cutting as it was done back in Texas, and Red showed them again and again. He cut out more cows with his single trained horse than any four Mexi-

77

cans on the job, but the boss was not there to see him and the *paisanos* kept on as before. They worked in pairs, and that divided their efficiency; their horses were "rode down," and that halved their efficiency again. Hour after hour the cutting dragged on, with the Mexicans still festive and gay. They cut, they trimmed herd and cut back again, until every petty rancher was satisfied.

The sun rose high and the "lonchas" were eaten; it sank low and they pulled in their belts; until, tired and hungry but still spurring their jaded mounts, the Mexicans turned back to camp. The various stray-herds were confined in different corrals, generally without a drop of water all night; and as the round-up moved on from place to place, Red watched, but he was beginning to lose interest. There were a thousand trails that the Mexicans knew, trails that he ought to learn, but he did not ride out with them now. The more he looked the proposition over, the more hopeless somehow it seemed.

"W'y, boys," he would say, "them Mexicans don't know *nothing*. I'd have to fire every one of 'em."

The big question was: Should he fire them and get Texans or should he let them have their own way? Roman was still smiling, his *muchachos* were always courteous, but Tex knew they would never change. They would always whirl a big loop and take their *dalavuelta* around the horn, where the Texans used a thirty-foot rope. They rode one horse till he was ready to drop, while the Texans would always change. But, worst of all, they were rough on the cattle— they "busted" them and chased them about. They left the stray-herd in the corral for twenty-four hours without giving them water or food. That was the way it had always been done.

But this was Red's problem, not ours, and after he had cleaned everybody that would shoot craps with him and out-lucked the Mexicans at monte, we left him to figure it out. To us the Mexicans seemed like very good people, taking life as it came without worrying too much about what the morrow would bring forth. If I had had my way I would have got them to singing ballads and soon been *buen amigo* with all of them, but as long as these Texans were around there was no use trying to be friends.

In a country where a white man would burn black in a month they were always drawing the color line and speaking of the Mexicans as "pies." That is all that is left of the word *paisano* after a Texan has chewed it up and spit it out; but it really means a countryman, a fellow citizen, and in Mexico is a term of respect. For a half-breed—half Mexican, half American—the Texans had something even worse. "Coyotes" they called them, a term of reproach in any language—and pronouncing it "kyotes" didn't help.

After being the guest of a man like Ramon Ahumada, I was, perhaps, a little prejudiced; but John Glissan and Leslie Wooddell, who had spent their lives among them, found the Mexicans very good friends. So we three got together, lying out under the stars, and mostly old John told mining stories. He was master of that droll exaggeration so characteristic of Western humor and he had rambled around so much among old-time frontiersmen that he had picked up a choice repertoire. One of his best was on Old Man Montgomery, a famous lion-hunter and liar, and I give it just as it came.

"Old Man Montgomery would go out into the hills for months, and all he would take for grub was a gunnysack full of white bread. When the dogs killed a lion he would cut out a chunk and eat that, and keep on until he met some old-timer who was qualified to appreciate his stories.

"He had camped down on Jim Yost and, while Jim was listening to a story that it took two hours to tell, he made up one of his own. Montgomery's stories were all about trailing mountain lions and the hand-to-hand fights he had with them, and Jim went on from there.

" 'I trailed a lion one time,' he said, 'until he wore off all his claws and had to den up in the rocks, but of course I went right in after him. Just as I turned the last corner a big rattlesnake raised his head and looked me in the eye, but I grabbed him by the neck, jumped in after the lion and, using the snake for a whip, I chased him clear out of there and across the plains to the San Pedro River.

The far tip of a great wave, moving across the West like a wall. Texas cowboys looking into Mexico. (*Photograph by Dane Coolidge*)

ROPING, MEXICAN STYLE.

Roman, the rodeo boss, ties his 60-foot *reata* to a calf, takes a turn around the horn, and brings it in on the trot.

(*Photograph by Dane Coolidge*)

" 'Well, did you ketch him?' says Montgomery, who didn't believe in spoiling a good story; and Jim Yost shook his head.

" 'When he got to the river,' he said, 'it was bone dry, but before I could start across a big cloudburst came down—a wall of water fifty feet high, sweeping everything before it—so of course I had to let him go.'

" 'That man is a dadburned liar,' says Montgomery. But I heard a bigger one than that. A feller was bragging about a rattlesnake he'd seen that was a hundred yards long and had rattles that looked like a string of box cars.

" 'Isn't that so, Bud?' he asked his pardner.

" 'Well, I don't know,' Bud says. 'It started to go down a hole before I got there and I only saw the last twenty-five feet.'

"I knew a Cousin Jack that was always telling about how deep the mines were in the old country, and another miner says:

" 'We have deep mines in this country, too. Out on the Mojave Desert I come to this camp, and you could see the top of the hoist twenty miles away. When I got close I saw a big cable running up to the wheel, but I couldn't see the engineer. He was down behind the drum, which was turning around real fast, asleep. I went down and woke him up and asked him when the cage would be up.

" 'Let's see,' he says. 'What day is this?'

" 'Tuesday,' I says.

" 'It'll be up at three-thirty, Thursday,' he says, and went to sleep again."

These came to him naturally, one after the other, and when he got tired of telling mining stories Cabezon would talk about cows. Or fighting his way into the Papago country while he looked for stolen stock. They lived in brush houses with a hole in one side for a door. At night when it was cold they would light a fire inside, and it was grand for the ones that were nearest but the boys on the outside nearly froze. They built a big corral around some lake or spring and trapped their horses and cattle during the dry months, May and June, before the summer rains set in.

Wooddell was sent out by the State Sanitary Board to report on stolen livestock, but he couldn't make any notes. The Indians were very suspicious of strangers and he had to remember all the brands. Even at that they spotted him for an officer. He wore his badge on the inside of his vest, under a sweater, but when he leaned over in a monte game a young Pima saw the edge of it gleam.

This boy rode ahead of him and told the Indians he was an officer, and they went inside and shut the door. He didn't know what was the matter and nearly died for water, but at last he broke into a house where they had four big *ollas* of it and took enough for himself and his horse. Then he noticed the boy's horse-track in the trail ahead and followed it until he caught up with him, and nearly scared him to death. After that the Indians let him alone.

The Papago sign for water is a round stone corral near the trail, with the opening towards the spring. In this opening they put from one to five small stones, which indicate by their number and size how far it is to water. The size of the corral itself indicates how much water there is, and when a trail is dry they make a picture of a man on a horse, to show that you will have to ride. A cross on a rock signifies a mine or mineral, not a grave. They were put over the first mines by the padres, who claimed all the gold for the Church.

The Papago sign for a brother is to hold the first fingers together. When they wish to indicate a sister, they make the same sign and touch the breasts. To say that a man is a coyote and treacherous they run their fingers up their knee like a fox trotting. To tell a man to mount and ride fast, they fork the right fingers over the left index finger, throw the right hand away from the body and snap the fingers. They speak slowly and correctly, when they condescend to talk at all.

"I—do—not—want—to—sell—all—my—cattle. I will—sell—one-hundred."

The Torres brothers, who had come to the round-up to claim their strays, were rich, for Indians, gathering a thousand head of cattle at one time when they trapped them in their big corral near San Miguel. They had a big stone house, with deer heads built into the walls so the horns would stick out and make hooks. They had good food, well served on tables, but would not invite a white man in and refused to come out after dark.

I had a rather scary experience while photographing these two Indians, who probably did not want their pictures taken, although they did not say so. In order to get them against the sky I dismounted and left my horse—one of the few times I worked on foot; and as I was going back to him somebody turned loose an old cow which had been trying to get away all the morning, and she caught me in the open.

There was no mistaking her intentions as she tossed her head and charged, but to the credit of the Papagos I will say that they never turned a hair. If this wild cow—which had been taken away from a place where her young calf was hiding and was therefore on the prod—happened to hook the picture-man in the ribs it was perfectly all right with them. If I had dropped my camera and made a run for it I could probably have beat her to the corral; but, rather than leave it for her to smash, I fell down on top of it and played "possum" until she finally went away. Nobody turned a hand to protect me from this old cow, which had horns as sharp and hooked as a billy goat's, and when I finally looked up the Papagos were still having a good laugh.

After that I was more careful about keeping my horse near me, where I could step up in a pinch, and

84

ROPING, TEXAS FASHION.
All good Texans use a 30-foot grass rope, tied to the horn; and they drag them in at a walk.
(*Photograph by Dane Coolidge*)

A Papago Indian on his dish-faced bronk. Black and silent and out for his rights.

(Photograph by Dane Coolidge)

CUTTING THE HERD

I was beginning to realize that nobody cared very much what happened to a Gringo photographer. A few days later, however, I was able to be of service to a vaquero who had had the first joint of his thumb pinched off when the turns of his dally "hopped." This is an experience not uncommon among the Mexicans—and the Americans who take their turns around the horn—and is one of the principal reasons why the Texans are so bitter against the *dalavuelta.* They tie their rope to the horn, and keep their hand away.

This poor man was suffering terribly and, as the Mexicans had no medicine along, he finally came to me. I had stayed in camp that day, and it had already become known that I carried a small stock of remedies. Among these was a favorite horse medicine, Hanford's Balsam of Myrrh, which quickly relieved the pain and, after I had bandaged the wound and supplied him with more balsam, I gave him a big drink. It was from a bottle that John Glissan always kept in his bed in case anybody got snake-bit, and the effect on the vaquero was magical.

He shook hands with me repeatedly and, when he found I could speak a little Spanish, sat down and told me all about it. Then he went to his horse, got a package of *pinole* meal from his saddlebags and gave it to me for a present. It was really a sign of friendship, and when the Mexicans came in from the rodeo their attitude had changed. The vaquero, who was a stray-man, had gone back to his ranch, but on the

85

way he had stopped long enough to tell them about that drink of whiskey. It came out then that he had had two or three already, that being the only medicine they had; but for a white man to rob his pardner to give a drink to a Mexican was something out of the ordinary.

Chapter IX

MEXICAN STORYTELLERS

They are great people—the Mexicans; and those who know them best like them best. At the same time they are different from Americans and there is no use trying to make them over. In their own way they have controlled most of the cattle country in the West for several hundred years, and they see no reason why they should change their ways to suit some Texano whom they despise.

Across the Line in Sonora and throughout Northern Mexico, there are Americans who have settled down and learned the ways of the country, and these men are full of stories about their faithful retainers —men who have worked for them for years and ask nothing better than to spend the rest of their lives on the ranch of some good *patrón*.

One of the most entertaining of these was Bisco Kibbey, a man of good family who had got into Sonora in a very peculiar way. After graduating from Harvard he went to Minnesota, where he spent the summer fishing and hunting until the weather began to get cold. Then he bought a big skiff, loaded it up with provisions and began to float down the Mississippi, looking for a place that was warmer.

The man who sold him the boat had told him that there were no obstacles in the river from there to New

Orleans, but one afternoon as he was floating along he saw a line, clear across the stream. Drifting nearer he noticed a house at each end of the line and decided that it must be a waterfall. There was a spillway on one side and Kibbey figured he could shoot it, but when he got almost there, he discovered a chain stretched across.

By this time he could see the tossing of the waves below the falls, where the water struck against some huge rocks, and he realized that to go over was sure death. So he turned his boat around, when he was within twenty feet of the edge, but found he could not make way against the current. He had been on the crew at Harvard, but the best he could do was to hold the boat even. If he had caught a crab he would have gone over the dam and been killed, but he fought his way clear across to the landing, tied up, and fainted away.

Kibbey floated on down the river and went clear to Cuba before he found a climate that was warm enough. Then he went on to Panama and started back overland until he came to the American Line. By doing this he qualified as a "Tropical Tramp," one of that strange, unorganized brotherhood composed of men who have rambled through Central America and Mexico, and he finally settled down in the Altar District of Sonora, where he established a large cattle ranch and lived a happy, carefree life.

On this ranch he had about a hundred Mexicans

BRANDING.

While two men hold the calf, a man with a hot running-iron burns the brand of its mother on its hip, while a fourth cuts the owner's earmark. Here we have two Mexicans, an American, and an Indian all working on the same calf.

(*Photograph by Dane Coolidge*)

CUTTING OUT THE BULL.

(Photograph by Dane Coolidge)

and one big, black Yaqui Indian. When Kibbey left home he gave the key of the storehouse to the Yaqui, and alway. found everything in good shape when he returned. For the first year the Indian worked for the regular wages—a peso and a half a day. After that Bisco told him he wouldn't pay him wages any more, but anything he wanted from the store he could have —money or anything else.

The Yaqui liked this and took less in a year than he had when he was drawing wages. He had a big family, and when they wanted any provisions they went and took them. When he needed a pair of overalls he took them, and once in a while he would draw five pesos and go off for a little time. He was a man about six feet two, with tremendous big hands and feet, like all of them, and small arms and legs. But the muscles in his arms and legs were like the sinews of a deer and he could outrun any horse on the ranch.

Kibbey handled the Mexicans in quite another way, but equally satisfactory to them—what he called the patriarchal system. They were so lazy and ornery he couldn't get more than a half a day's work out of them anyway, so he soaked them at the store, took every cent they earned away from them in trade, and paid them top wages—a peso and a half a day.

He sold them coffee at a peso and a half a kilo, which meant a fifty per cent profit for him, and everything else in proportion, but he never drove them at their work, never scolded them or spoke roughly to them, and they seemed glad to keep on working for nothing. One thing he would never do was to let them get in debt to him, as that made them very disgruntled on the one hand, and made them think he was afraid to fire them, on the other. So when one of his Mexicans got in debt to the store he would cross it off the books and tell him to get busy again.

Living among them for years he had learned a great deal about their ways of handling stock, which were those of the old-time Mexicans, and on his visits to Nogales he told me some wonderful stories. Not only of conditions in Mexico, where the revolution made living dangerous; but folk stories, handed down by professional storytellers or told around the fires. In most of these the Gachupin, or Spaniard, is the butt, much as the Englishman used to be in the United States; although as a matter of fact, the Spanish could think circles around them.

One time a Mexican cowboy was riding along a trail ahead of a Spaniard when he encountered a long limb which he caught hold of to make way for him. But the Spaniard was so slow in coming up that the vaquero was compelled to release the limb, which struck him between the eyes and knocked him off his horse. Yet, instead of becoming angry, the Gachupin rushed forward and insisted upon shaking hands.

"Brother," he said, "you have saved my life. If you had not held that limb back it would have killed me."

Mexican Storytellers

A Spaniard, an Indian, and a Mexican were out prospecting on the desert when they discovered a rich deposit of gold and worked at it desperately until dark. They then found that the burro upon which their provisions had been packed, and which in their excitement they had forgotten to unsaddle, had left them and headed back to their last camp, twenty or thirty miles away.

As it was dark they could not follow its trail and they did not know what to do until the Mexican suggested a solution. During the day a dove had lit by the water-hole and he had killed it with a rock. This was the only food they had and he hung it up on a limb, saying:

"We will keep this dove until morning and go to sleep; and the man who has the best dream shall then eat the dove and start out after the burro, and to bring help, while the other two shall stay behind and starve along until he returns."

In the morning as soon as it was light they awoke and the Indian spoke right up:

"I had a fine dream," he said. "I dreamed that I died and went to heaven; and Saint Peter received me and asked me what I wanted. I told him I wanted something to eat and he took me down a long hall where there were lots of different rooms and showed me a fine table with all kinds of food on it, and I sat there and ate and ate. I tell you, it was a fine dream and I think I ought to have the dove."

"I had a fine dream too," said the Spaniard. "I dreamed I went to heaven and Saint Peter took me down that same hall. I saw Pedro in a room, stuffing himself with grub, but Saint Peter took me past there to another very beautiful hall, where there was not only plenty of food but fine wine and beautiful flowers, with music and girls to wait on me, and I think I ought to have the dove."

Then the Mexican said:

"I also dreamed that I went to heaven and Saint Peter took me down that same hall. I saw Pedro in there, stuffing himself with grub, and the Gachupin drinking wine and listening to the music. But Saint Peter took me further down the hall and he was going to give me something wonderful, but just then somebody called him away, and as he did not come back and I saw you boys had everything you wanted, I got up and ate the dove."

Two Mexican vagabonds were walking the streets of Hermosillo the morning after a big drunk and feeling very *crudo*, when they looked in a doorway and saw a man stretched out on the floor, the way the Mexicans "wake" their dead. Some people were sitting around, and there was a bottle of mescal. So the vagabonds joined the circle and got several good drinks.

As the night came on the friends of the deceased went away. Then his relatives departed and finally his

Mexican *paisano*, or countryman, called a "pie" by the Texans. They ride the same horse all day.

(Photograph by Dane Coolidge)

A rush for freedom. After wild cattle have been shut up all day they pour out of the gate like a torrent and sometimes run several miles.

(*Photograph by Dane Coolidge*)

wife and parents, but as there was still nearly a bottle of mescal left, the two vagabonds remained. After a drink or two, one said to the other:

"Well, what shall we do until morning?" And the other said:

"Why not tell stories?"

Now the first vagabond had only one eye and the second had only one leg, so the one-legged man said:

"All right, how did you come to lose your eye?"

"Well," said El Tuerto, "that is a long story and it makes me very sad. I fell in love with a very beautiful woman and married her, but I was tortured by the fear that she was unfaithful to me; so one day, in order to satisfy my doubts, I told her that I would visit my parents in Magdalena.

"That evening I went down and took the train, but at the first station I got off and walked back to my house. Sure enough, there was a light in my wife's bedroom and in great excitement I crept up and looked through the keyhole. But some clothes were hung over a chair in front of it and I could not see. Neither could I see through the crack of the door.

"I thought then of looking through the transom, but as you see I am a very short man and, as there was nothing for me to stand on, I took out this eye and held it up to the transom. There, instead of another man, I beheld my poor wife sitting upon the bed and weeping over my picture. This so agitated me that I ran from the house and clear to the railroad station, resolved that she should never know of my suspicions. But in my excitement I still carried my eye in my hand, and when I reached the station it was so cold and had swelled up so that I could never get it back."

The one-legged man now spoke up and said:

"Yes, that was a very sad thing to happen, but I lost my leg in the service of my country at the battle of Puebla. At that time my commander had less than a thousand men within the city walls and the enemy were so close about us that not even a dog could slip through the lines. We were in a very desperate situation as we were separated from our friends on the outside, and if we did not get help that day we would be lost. But if we could send word to our friends to attack from the rear and draw off most of their forces, our commander was sure he could cut his way out. So he lined us all up in the plaza and said:

" '*Muchachos,* we are in great peril and unless I can get a message to our friends on the hill yonder we are lost. This will be so dangerous that I will not order any of you to undertake the mission but I will call for volunteers.'

"At that every one of those brave men stepped forward and the commander was very much pleased.

" 'But,' he said, 'I cannot choose from so many brave men.'

"So he had us draw lots, and the mission fell to me. Now I knew that this was a very hazardous undertaking and before consulting with my commander I bade

94

all my comrades farewell. He then led me to a single great cannon which he had there and explained his plan in detail.

" 'You must stand by the mouth of this cannon,' he said, 'and when the ball comes out you must seize it and ride with it over the camp of the enemy and into the camp of our friends.'

"So I stood ready and, when the cannon ball came out, I caught a good hold of it and got up on top of it. As I flew over the camp of the enemy they saw me and began shooting, but I thumbed my nose at them and rode on, straight for the camp of our friends. The commander had indeed aimed well, for I saw I should fall in their midst. But as I came closer I perceived that the cannon ball was heading for a great mesquite stump, about ten feet high and rough and hard as iron. In order to deflect its course I pulled off my hat and held it behind as a rudder, but the cannon ball was going so fast that the most I could do was to save my head, and the tree trunk took off this leg."

At this the dead man rose up from his place and said:

" 'This is too much. If you boys are going to tell any more stories like that I am going to lie down in the other room.' "

Every Mexican in the District of Altar has a mine or *prospecto* to sell, and one of them found such a good one that he said he would not part with it for less than a million dollars. At last an American, who knew the ignorance of the Mexicans, told him he would pay that if it was good. Then he went to Guaymas and bought a thousand dollars' worth of pesos, half pesos, twenty-cent pieces, and dimes and brought it back in a canvas bag.

When the Mexican was near the location of the mine he stopped and told the American to first show him the million dollars.

"All right," said the American and, after spreading a blanket on the ground, he emptied the big bag of silver upon it. The Mexican then began to count, but when he got up to fifty pesos he said he would have to get his brother, who could count better than he could. The brother came and counted up to ninety. Then he quit, saying he was sure that such a big pile was all of a million dollars. So the American got the mine for a thousand dollars.

Bisco Kibbey had a Mexican cattle-buyer who couldn't write his own name, but he was shrewd in dealing with the natives. One time when they were out buying they met a Mexican on the trail who had about fifty head of cattle, one-third of which were yearlings and two-year-olds, but the remainder were fine big steers. Ramon, the cattle-buyer, offered thirty pesos apiece for the big stuff, but the Mexican insisted that he ought to give him thirty pesos a head for all of them.

Ramon finally offered him twenty pesos a head for the little stuff, but the Mexican held out stubbornly for thirty.

"I'll tell you what I will do," said Ramon, "if you will yoke them together in *manieros,* or pairs, a big one and a little one, I will give you forty-five pesos a pair."

The Mexican struck for forty-eight, and they finally compromised at forty-six and shook hands on the bargain. Then the Mexican yoked his smallest calf to a steer and received his forty-six dollars for them, but in a short time all his little stuff was gone and he had nothing but big steers left. He tried to get out of it then, but Ramon told him it was his own fault and he would have to go through with the bargain, for he had shaken hands on it. So the Mexicans yoked the smallest ones he had with the big ones until they were all paired off, and he had to take a big loss for trying to be so smart.

Chapter X

MEXICAN HORSE BREAKERS

THE Sonora Mexicans figure on breaking a horse in six or seven hours where it would take a white man that many days. But they treat them rough, of course, and often break their spirit. One man ropes the horse by the neck, the other ropes him by the hind legs and they stretch him out on the ground while they put a *tapojo,* or blind, over his eyes. Then they put a *jáquima,* a rawhide halter, on him and jerk the rough nosepiece around until it makes his nose very sore. After that they get him up and saddle him and he stands with his legs far apart, trembling.

They pull his head around to one side, to loosen up his neck, and tie it there for an hour or so, then tie it up on the other side. Putting the *tapojo* on again, so they can mount, one and often two men climb up on him. They jerk him to one side by his sore nose to teach him to rein, then jerk him the other way as he runs. Then, while one of the riders pulls his head to one side, they swing their weight the other way and throw him down.

After spurring and riding him a while they gallop out into the country, with a vaquero following along behind to head him one way or the other. When they have ridden him down they bring him back to the ranch and, as a test, to see whether he is broke, they tie a load of cut grass on his back, where it will hang down and tickle his flanks. If he carries it nicely he is broke.

When a band of wild horses can be caught in no other way, fifty or sixty Mexicans round them up and drive them under a broad tree, in the branches of which a man had been hidden, with many ropes. As the horses mill around beneath the tree they never look up and the man puts the loop of a *reata* on the end of a stick and drops it over one of their heads. He then throws the other end to some vaquero, who either catches it in the air or picks it up as it drags and leads the horse away.

But not all Mexicans break their horses in this rough and brutal way and there are many who fairly love their pets. Bisco Kibbey owned a horse named Noviero, or Steer Catcher, which had been broken by a half-locoed Mexican named Ramon, who would not sell him at any price. The first time Kibbey saw Noviero, Ramon was riding him on the dead run down a steep, rocky hill, with the reins in his lap and shooting a 30-30 rifle at a bunch of buro deer—he killed two of them, too. And besides being a wonderful running-horse, Noviero had been taught many tricks.

When Ramon was drunk and falling down over his neck, the horse would always move over, to keep under him, and if he fell off Noviero would stand beside him until he woke up. He was also taught to take

99

a standing jump over rocks and fences and, while he was ordinarily slow and had a very rough trot, he had never gone after a steer without catching him. All that was necessary was to turn him loose and he would follow the steer anywhere, with the reins on his neck.

He would trot sixty or eighty miles in a day or night over any kind of country, and his gallop was very easy. Ramon had broken him and another horse just like him. They were sorrels, with white manes and tails, wonderfully muscled in the shoulders and legs, and the only reason Kibbey was ever able to buy Noviero was that his master had ridden him too hard. When he was drunk he would race him over the rocks until he got sand-cracks in his hoofs and had to be put out to pasture.

Then Kibbey bought him for two hundred dollars, gold—a very high price for a sound horse—and took him to an old Mexican who was a kind of horse doctor. This doctor cut two big notches in his hoofs, above the cracks and near the hair, so deep that the blood ran out, and turned him loose on bosky ground. His hoofs were so injured by this treatment that he finally shed them, and four or five months later he had an entirely new set.

Bisco would not sell him at any price, for he could outrun any horse in the country and he depended upon him to save his life when the *insurrectos* came. When General Campo and his bandits were raiding through the country, Kibbey did all his riding in the nighttime. The superstitious Mexicans are not only afraid to travel at night but they are afraid of everything they see at night, and as long as he could keep them from stealing his horse he felt safe.

In some way Kibbey had got hold of the brother of Noviero and kept him in a stable across the Line; but Ramon cried and begged for him so much, saying he could not live without him, that Kibbey told him he would give the horse back. When they entered the stable Ramon rushed at the *noviero* and grabbed him around both hind legs; but instead of kicking his head off—which he would have done for anybody else—the horse just turned his head and looked at him.

These horses were probably of the same blood as the famous golden horses which Queen Isabella sent to Mexico, and wherever they have gone for thousands of years men have loved them as did Ramon. The beautiful Rayo del Sol, which Pancho Villa had just ridden into Nogales, was another of the royal blood, the *sangre azul* of the horse world. While stolen again and again they have always been spared and prized for their grace and speed, and they have brought many a man to his doom.

Unfortunately for Ramon he enlisted in the Rurales, the Rangers of Mexico, shortly before the Constitutionalists forced them and their Cossack leader, Colonel Kosterlitzky, to cross the Line into Arizona. There were wild times in Nogales when the Constitutionalist Army closed in on the town; and the citizens of Nogales, Sonora, made the mistake of hooting Kosterlitzky, before he crossed and surrendered. To avenge himself for these insults the Cossack commander drew his sword and, at the head of his fighting men, charged back at the rabble, leaving many of them dead in the street. Then he rode to the Line and surrendered his bloody sword to the Americans.

Ramon was there with the rest, but so solicitous was he for the safety of Noviero that he locked him up in a house—on the Mexican side. When he crossed, to be interned, he told Kibbey where Noviero was and Bisco engaged a Mexican boy that he knew to slip across and bring him out. According to the rules of war, the mounts of the Rurales were to be seized and held for the Federals; but when the boy returned he told the United States Customs guards that the horse belonged to Kibbey. They telephoned up to the hotel where Bisco stopped and, learning that he was in town, they let Noviero pass.

So he was saved from the hands of the Constitutionalists and, as Kibbey expected Ramon to be released in a few days, he kept his horse for him for several months. But when Ramon was interned at Camp Rosecrans, California, he was compelled to release the horse to the Mexican Federal Government, and Kibbey had to give it up. He was taken with the other mounts to Calabasas, Arizona, but a short time later Bisco heard a ranchman boasting about the fine little horse he had saved from that bunch of Federal mounts.

Once more—as had happened to the *palomillos* through thousands of years of war—Noviero had changed hands and, still proud and aloof, aware of his regal blood and the respect it had always won, he passed on to another master. When Ramon was paroled he undoubtedly came back to seek out his beloved Noviero, and a little job of horse-stealing would not stand between him and the horse without which he could not live. And Bisco, judging from the look in his eye when he spoke of the boastful rancher, was drifting the same way.

Chapter XI

WAR!

I HAD not been in the Baboquivari Valley a week when the "lasting peace" which had been signed at Nogales was smashed to smithereens. Villa snatched General Obregon off the train at Chihuahua City while he was passing through to the City of Mexico and, but for the protests of all his advisors, would have put him up against the wall. As it was, though reluctantly, he let him take the night train south, then wired ahead to a trusted general to take him off and kill him. But Obregon had a hunch before he reached the first station and, pulling the bell-rope, he dropped off and disappeared into the night.

Now the war was going on worse than ever, with the Yaquis trying to take Naco, not a hundred miles east, and a big battle all along the Line. New war tariffs were being imposed—and export duties to keep the cattle from being shipped out of Mexico; but day by day in a resistless flood they came pouring across the Line. With a big demand for beef in this country on account of the war in Europe, the price even for Mexican cattle had gone up to fifty dollars a head. But behind all this exporting was the fear on the part of Sonora cattlemen that the revolution was about to close down upon them again and they would lose every cow that they had.

War!

The Yaqui Indians had broken loose from Governor Maytorena and taken over half the state, and they are great meat eaters. I have seen a big steer driven down the street of Nogales, Sonora, and turned over to a band of Yaqui soldiers and five minutes later all that was left was a bloody spot on the ground and the contents of the paunch. There was no waste—they used everything—but they used lots of it.

This turmoil just across the Line had a very disquieting effect on the Mexicans, especially as Texas cattle-buyers were swarming in to buy the cows as soon as they were crossed—every man like Red Tex with a high-crowned hat and a pistol on his hip. At Nogales the United States sanitary inspectors were a week behind on their work and, on account of the war conditions below the Line, many cattle were allowed to cross at Sásabe. It was only in the districts south and west of central Sonora that fever ticks were known to exist and stock from within the sanitary district was being rushed across.

When seized on the American side for evasion of duty the cattle were often sold for taxes, and several cowmen got their start by buying them in cheap. From the border, the feeders were shipped north to Wyoming and Montana, or west to the Imperial Valley and the rich pastures of Central California. But, no matter who the ultimate purchaser might be, the buyers were Texans to a man, and that looked bad to the Mexicans.

Our Arizona Ranger and a Sanitary Inspector had gone over into Papaguería, to investigate complaints from different cattle companies that the Indians were stealing their beef. But they were met at the pass by four armed Papagos, who rode guard on them as they passed from town to town. They finally came to a village where a cactus-pear fiesta was going on and all the Indians had got drunk on the wine.

Being given ten minutes to leave town, the Americans took the back trail. But, after their guards left them, they turned around—with a posse of eleven cowboys—and re-arrested a Papago, whom they had caught butchering company beef. Over forty Papagos surrounded them, with rifles in their hands, and followed them for several miles; but the officers refused to give up their prisoner and the Indians went back to their wine.

Things had quieted down a little by the time we had crossed the valley to Ronstadt's Ranch, and there Red Tex and his friend decided to put on a grandstand play. Near the summit of the peak there was a tank in the rocks where wild cattle drank after the rains, and the Mexicans had never been able to catch them. But at the present price of beef those old mossheads were worth big money and—just to show how it was done back in Texas and win a further stand-in with the Boss—Ronstadt's Texan took four or five cowboys and rode up on the rocky peaks.

It was rough work and they went hungry, besides

The Yaqui Indians are good soldiers, but they eat a lot of beef. Five minutes after a steer has been driven into their camp there is nothing left but the contents of the paunch.

(Photograph by Dane Coolidge)

PANCHO VILLA.

With a cactus-tree saddle and the best horse he could find in Mexico. He is wearing the *mitajas,* or *taja* leggins, and bull-snout *tapaderos.*

sleeping out overnight, but the next morning at dawn they started a drive and brought in eighteen head. That showed what a Texan can do. They put these wild cattle into a stout corral and lashed the bars together with a *reata*, but the next morning every cow was gone. That shows what a Mexican can do. I wondered if by any chance that gate could have been unlashed by the three vaqueros who had been fired when the first Texan came.

Here was something for Red Tex to think over, before he brought out his family and settled down to run the La Osa outfit. But Ronstadt's Texan took it hard. Instead of winning a stand-in with the Boss he had lost over a thousand dollars' worth of cows and got the Mexicans so they would hardly speak. He had shown what a rancher could expect when he laid off all his Mexican hands and tried to work the cattle "right." As he looked at it this was spite work on the part of the "pies"—although it took only one man to turn the cattle loose—and he was bitter in his remarks.

As for Red, he stopped riding out with the Mexicans and evidently had something on his mind. Perhaps he was lonely, for he was a long way from Texas, and we "white folks" would soon be gone. Or perhaps he was thinking of just what would happen if he fired all the La Osa hands. Would they retire to their canyons and look on politely while he worked the range with a few Texans; or would they, for instance, unlash the gates at night and turn all his cattle loose! It was a difficult problem for Red and he no longer took notice when the Mexicans busted a cow.

The round-up dragged along as always, with such a circle of "pies" around the herd that they could hardly cut out the cows; and it was a battle to get to the grub. At the same time the Mexicans were politer than ever, and when Roman's wife sent him down a sack of cakes, he showed us the courtesy of his people. These cakes were folded over, with a yellow filling in the middle which made Rye Miles call them "pay-streak cakes"; and when our mayordomo saw us watching him he rode over and gave every man a cake.

That is Spanish hospitality, which dictates that in the presence of others, a man cannot eat or drink until he has offered what he has to the rest. This is often a mere formality, a perfunctory gesture which no one is expected to accept; but Roman insisted, although the Texans hardly knew how to take it. Red Tex accepted and thanked him, but Ronstadt's man was still black with hate. At the same time this spontaneous generosity made us feel that Roman, at least, was our friend; and things went along very nicely until we moved back across the valley—and it rained.

We were camped at Secondino's, a deep well equipped with a pump, and after the storm the Mexicans were so happy that they began to sing again. All along I had wished to hear their round-up song, which they composed every year as the rodeo progressed, a verse for every man. Their last one was called "*Viente-quatro de Mayo*," "The Twenty-fourth of May," the date when the spring round-up had begun; and when we heard their shouts of laughter I went over with Cabezon and asked Roman to repeat it for us.

As the ground was very muddy we had thrown down some brush by the fire upon which to spread our blankets; and when Roman, with two others, came over after supper we looked forward to a very good time. Just the three Mexicans and the three Americans—the Texans being still rated another race of men; but as the singing went on they appeared out of the darkness and sat down with the rest of the Gringos.

Roman would start off in a high tenor, or falsetto; then Carlos would join in with the alto and burly Rico would sing the bass. I had heard the same kind of part songs in Spain and was listening very intently when, without any reason, Ronstadt's Texan reached out and kicked the ends of the burning sticks. The sparks flew in the air and while we were kicking them off our blankets, he set up such a howl of laughter that I told him to shut up.

Things quieted down then and the Mexicans, having begun the song, went on as if nothing had happened; but they had just got to going again when our bad Texan let out another whoop. He leaped up, kicking the fire and scattering the coals; and in the excitement I said several things which I should, perhaps, have regretted. Roman and his friends rose up, wished us all *buenos noches* and left, but Ronstadt's Texan was still on the prod.

"What do you mean?" he demanded, following after me with his hand on his gun. "I want you to understand, suh, I don't allow no man to tell me to hush up!"

He meant it, too; so I begged his pardon. And, when he started in all over, I begged his pardon again. He was waiting, of course, for me to refuse to apologize; and this sudden meekness, induced by the six-shooter, saved me from getting hurt. He turned and went away, without any more ranikaboo plays, and the next morning he was all right again, although Red was badly hacked. He quit a few days later and went back to Texas, but if Roman was glad you would never have known it.

Shortly afterwards we moved on to Punta de Agua and began working the Arivaca range, and John Glissan released some of his best Texas stories which he had hesitated to spring on Red. Ronstadt's Texan had gone home and there was no one to put up a fight. The people around Arivaca were glad to see us back again; and Beanie Bogan, the storekeeper, began where John left off. He was from California, the land of small matches and big liars, and what he had to say about Texas was scandalous. Then Jack McVey rode down from Las Jarillas, and Rye Miles capped the climax.

Jack was quite a character around Arivaca, he being our only dude cowboy and Ramon Ahumada's pet. With another Eastern boy he had come to Arizona and started to rough it in style. After building a frontier castle that was the wonder of the countryside, he had brought out Will and Mandy, his faithful colored servants, to cook and mix the drinks. Every time they got lonely for a little colored society he would give them a trip to Tucson—the rest of the time it was open house.

The castle was furnished in the most expensive manner, with a big Persian rug in the living room that had cost around thirty thousand dollars. To keep from wearing holes in this exquisite work of art, boards were laid across it for the cowboys to walk on, and the drinks were always on tap. The year before, Jack's partner had been killed while riding a bronk, and since then Jack's enthusiasm for the Wild Western life had suffered and his roping had fallen off.

This had been very noticeable the day before when he had gone in to drag out calves, and Rye Miles was waiting for him.

"Say, boys," he began, "how many throws did Jack make yesterday, when he tried to ketch that calf? There was nothing but Texans around, and they can't count above a hundred, so I never did rightly know."

That called for another round of drinks on Jack, but he took it like a sport.

Another character in whom they took pride at Arivaca was old Porfirio, the honest Mexican. In his youth he had been caught while working over some brands for his master, but he had begged so hard that the posse had spared his life. Since then and for forty years Porfirio had never altered a brand, and when any allusion was made to his former dereliction he would cross his thumb over his first finger and, kissing it like a cross, cry out:

"Por esta cruz, I have never stolen another cow!"

This was all the more notable from the fact that his brother had the reputation of being the worst "coyote" in the country.

Everybody was friendly in old Arivaca, and with the Texans out of the way, the nights were spent in music and song and dancing with the gay señoritas. But I never did get the words of "The Twenty-fourth of May" which the boys had been singing by the fire; and when, twenty-five years later, I returned to Arivaca, the good old days were gone.

Ramon was dead and Roman was dead, and the Texans had taken over the range. In all that country there was only one outfit where the Mexicans sang as they worked, and it was far back in the mountains, without even a road leading in. Arivaca looked

WAR!

strange, but on the highway near Tubac I found my friend Carmen Zepeda. She told me how Roman had lost all his money by betting on a horse race and had passed away, very poor. And our old friend, Ramon, who had given so lavishly to his *compadre* and helped out all who came, had been injured by a fall from his horse and had never got back his strength. He too had died poor. They were all poor now, she said, and nobody sang—there was really nothing to sing for.

But these vaqueros who still sang by the fire at night—perhaps they could write down some songs! They had been such beautiful songs—the old *corridos* —and soon they too would be gone. They would all be forgotten, along with the brave days when the cowboys came to the rodeo, every man with a fine horse and saddle, and silver on his bit and spurs.

Carmen agreed to try, and here are the songs. A little strange as to spelling and full of allusions to things that happened long ago, but Mexican *corridos,* like the ballads of Old Spain.

Chapter XII

CORRIDOS

Corrido Para Valerio Quintero

Voy a cantar un corrido
lo canto con desespero
ese corrido es compyesto
para Valerio Quintero

Dice Valerio Quintero
Que era hombre y no se negaba
por donde quiera que andaba
la gente lo respetaba

Dice Valerio Quintero
que le importa muy poquito
matar a un compadre de pila
en ese batanealito

Cuando llegaron al rio
Valerio llegó primero
les dice a sus compañeros
pues adonde está el dinero

Dice Valerio Quintero
oyga don Jose Maria
necesito tres mil pesos
antes que amanezca el dia.

"CORRIDOS"

Dice don Jose Maria
valgame Dios que será esto
lo que me pidas "balerio"
lo que me pides te presto

Y se metió para dentro
por que Valerio le exije
muy pronto le metió parque
auna carabina y un rifle

Dice don Jose Maria
ya te los voy a prestar
y de adentro para fuera
luego le empezo a tirar

El primer tiro ledió
yse lo atinó en un muzlo
y alli se cayo Valerio
despidiendose del mundo

Luego que vio Valerio
Que remedio no tenia
levanta la vista al Cielo
Viva la Virgen Maria

El compañero que traia
no lo quiso ver penar
le dió un balazo en la frente
y lo acabo de matar

OLD CALIFORNIA COWBOYS

Ya con ésta me despido
por la via de un estero
aqui se acaba el corrido
de don Valerio Quintero

Corrido of Valerio Quintero

Translations by Gregorio Artieda

I am going to sing a *corrido*
I sing it with desperation
This *corrido* is composed
For Valerio Quintero.

Said Valerio Quintero
Who was a man, it cannot be denied,
Who wherever he went
Was respected by the people.

Said Valerio Quintero
It mattered little to him
To kill a *compadre de pila* [1]
In case of a rough-house.

When they arrived at the river
Valerio got there first
And he said to his companions
Now where is the money?

[1] Two who bear the relationship of godfather and father to a child.

"CORRIDOS"

Said Valerio Quintero
Listen, Don Jose Maria,
I need three thousand pesos
Before the dawn of day.

Said Don Jose Maria
For God's sake what is this
What you ask me is *balerio* [2]
What you ask me I will give you.

And he went inside
Because Valerio was insistent
And quickly with bullets
He loaded a carbine and a rifle.

Said Don Jose Maria
These I am going to give you
And aiming outward from within
At once he began to shoot.

The first shot he gave him
He struck him in the thigh
And there fell Valerio
Bidding farewell to the world.

Then when Valerio saw
That remedy there was none
He lifted his eyes to heaven
Saying Long live the Virgin Mary.

[2] A quantity of bullets.

The companion he brought with him
Unwilling to see him suffer more
Gave him a shot in the forehead
And finished killing him.

Now with this I say good-bye
As I leave by the creek
Here ends the *corrido*
Of Don Valerio Quintero.

Corrido De El Merino Mentado

Corrido of Merino, the Boaster

Listen, you famous Merino,
Is your heart heavy?
Because you seem to be crushed
Or is the opinion false
That they have of you in Tucson
That you are master of the situation?

Are you not that braggart
That goes about making such a noise
Are you not the strong champion
Of those who take your part.
How much do you really appreciate
The fame that you have lost?

But are you now convinced
As to your exploits of the past
That you did not deserve the credit?

"CORRIDOS"

Have you stopped to consider that in the game
All that you had lost
Was won back merely by chance?

We have all made up our minds
That you should not go on
Because if further bragging of yours
Should get you compromised
You would find yourself in a hole
And, God help us, what would we do then?

I am going to make you understand
That what you do from now on
On any ground that you may choose
I am going to throw down the gauntlet
Just to make you understand
That I can meet you face to face.

I can't see you as a soldier
You have nothing of the warrior
I only figure you as a hypocrite
To be kept crushed down
And I am not a man who changes his mind
Quick as I am on the draw, there is nothing to fear.

I belong to the crew of the penniless
And go sailing before the wind
The bets have been small
And you are getting tired of winning
Though you crave money
And fear makes you tremble.

Old California Cowboys

Do not go about bragging again
Neither look about for small coins
Nor go out prospecting
Without knowing about metals.
There is no mine more valuable
Than that of Tomas Gonzales.

He has money and animals
Always ready for a fight
And between the posts that mark
The boundaries of his mine
There are tons and tons of hay.

If you don't like the boss you have,
Order another one at Sonora
One who will treat you better.
Rosalio is mine now
Always disposed to fight
Who cries out even in his solitude.

Your crowd is disposed to bet
Only when they feel so inclined
But as they see a customer coming
They don't want to gamble now.
Because they talk like parrots
And all shrinks down to size of a dwarf.

The flag of Mexico
You should not defile
Have respect for the Republicans

"CORRIDOS"

As the liberal party.
Because the patriot for profit
Is a legal party.

A great clamor proclaimed
The candlesticks and the cross
Help me, doña Maria,
Antonio Jesus has not died
But is certainly dying
And will be left without light.

Corrido of The Twentieth of January

There is going to be a race
On the twentieth of January
They are going to put up the bay horse
Against my light weight.

I shall be there with the others
And shall be very quiet
Watching to see if this horse wins for me
As he did over the black.

Because it certainly will not happen
As the backers of the bay predict
That I shall be standing motionless
At the time of the signal for starting.

I rode close beside the other horse
To see if he really had a chance
Being that all his backers
Had every confidence in him.

OLD CALIFORNIA COWBOYS

Now they have lost all hope
Of winning against my bay
They will have to put on him
The hoofs of some other horse!

Don't believe that I am so far wrong
Or that I am steeped in indigo
For playing them a race
Like that of Juan Vigil.

If they don't want to do it for themselves
Let them do it for their horse
Until they cry "enough"
Here we have it, no fooling.

If there yet remains yeast
Save it for making bread
So you can play the races
In company with don Juan.

Corrido of Lorenzo Cabral

In eighteen hundred and eight
Pedro Soto when all is told
Was the cause of the death
Of Lorenzito Cabral.

Say I to my friends
Let the matter rest there
Pedro Soto was the cause
Of the death of Cabral.

"Corridos"

Perhaps he never had been
Arrested, killed, or badly wounded
But I don't let this bother me
He had had suffering enough.

When you go down to the lakes
Don't you go and forget
To bring me as prisoners
Benito and this Lorenzo Cabral.

This bunch of cattle is very much mine
And where it grazes, too,
Why then did they take it away
And with whose permission?

Off rode the band of vaqueros
With a hell of a stir
Because they were going to lasso
At the ranch of Pedro Soto.

Vaqueros and their leaders
All skilled in the use of the lasso
Take me out of this desert
This is the last favor I ask.

The horse that was once yours
Is neither pinto nor bay
He is a sorrel horse
Bearing a lawyer's brand.

OLD CALIFORNIA COWBOYS

I do not grieve for my silver-mounted saddle
Nor for my handsome colts
But I do grieve for my horse
That he should be in the hands of another.

Fly, fly, little dove,
Tire not with flying
Here ends the *corrido*
Of one Lorenzo Cabral.

Corrido of Jose Lisorio

Sunday it surely was
That this affair took place
The day when Jose Lisorio
Gave a beating to his mother.

So infuriated was the mother
She hurled a curse at him
At the very foot of a crucifix
So that the earth itself trembled.

"I hope in the names of God and Mary
(And may the saints also hear me)
That when you go down in the mine
You will be crushed into a thousand pieces."

Off to the mine he went to work
Sad and most disconsolate
Thinking of the malediction
That his mother had heaped upon him.

"Corridos"

Mother of mine, who gave me life,
Lift from me your malediction
The son of your womb I am
And blood of your very heart.

He went down the first step
And from there he prayed:
"You of the Holy Name, take care of me
From the cross on which You died."

He went down the second step
And from there he fell far down.
Companions that were with him
Took him out, laid on a blanket.

Greatly frightened they were
And one took off his lamp
And said to the foreman:
"One of our companions has been killed."

His brains were gathered up
In the crown of a hat
The sight was enough to soften
Even a heart of steel.

They bore him away from the mine
And laid him down near a wall.
May those of the Holy Names pity him
And his soul achieve forgiveness.

They wrapped him up in a blanket
And to the cemetery carried him
His mother, on seeing him pass
Hurled her malediction at him again.

Like a drop of dew
Like a sip of honey and wine
Has the said Jose Lisorio
Disappeared with the passing wind.

This *corrido* of the race of the Pinta mare and Roman's striped horse was made to Roman Acebeda by his admirers, the ranchers of Arivaca, for whom he won lots of money. In another race Roman lost all he had, including the horse, although his wife begged him not to bet; and his friends lost their money too.

Corrido of the Race of the Pinta (spotted mare)
and the Rayado (striped horse)

At the Fair in Nogales
On Sunday the sixth of May
There was run the race
Of the Pinta and the Rayado.

When they called the start
The Pinta was off on the instant
But before half the course was run
The Rayado was ahead.

"Corridos"

"Here now," said the Rayado
To the Pinta, in firm tones,
"It's no use for you to exert yourself,
There at the rope I'll wait for you!"

I am the Striped Horse
Come all the way from Arivaca
To do up the Pinta
Together with all her backers.

Now you have lost the races
You thought to win
I told you it would come out this way
So do not race me any more.

Now then, you lively Pinta,
All played out, but given to fancies,
They will not be so fair spoken
Now that they have lost the race.

They would have had something to say
Had it come out either way
They say now that your champion
Must have sold out the race.

Don't say I'm unduly elated
Because I have won this race
Well you know that I am your daddy
In Arizona and Sonora.

OLD CALIFORNIA COWBOYS

As to the race just run
There is no doubt now
That you were too young,
Besides, you were with foal.

I know you can't be used for the lasso
Neither can you race.
Tell your master, Sienas,
To take you over to Altar.

There, if you can, get them
To go on with your training
I myself need no schooling
Neither does Rosario Valenzuela.

For the Pinta, an accordion
I have already brought
To be given to Basilio
So he can play the Charleston for her.

Don't think that I am a poet
I am but an amateur
That is why I sing this refrain!
For the Striped Horse, Hurray!

My first name is Cipriano,
My good humor knows no end
Attention to the wants of all,
Ortega, your good friend.

THREE: COWBOYS IN OLD MEXICO

Chapter XIII

THE CONQUERORS

WHEN Cortés, with 553 men and sixteen horses, landed on the coast of New Spain, it was the horses that conquered Mexico. With thousands of trained warriors, the Aztec squadrons charged in to drive them from their shores and for an hour the battle raged. But, even against their cannon, the Indians fought on, throwing dust into the air to conceal the number of their dead; until suddenly, from their rear, the horsemen appeared, and Montezuma's army fled.

They thought the rider and the horse were one body—some strange, supernatural creature sent out to destroy them—and during the invasion that followed it was always the horses that won. Armed with swords and lances the cavalry swept down on them, and when the Spaniards lost a horse, they wept. One horse was worth ten men. They were beautiful creatures, all trained for war, and Bernal Diaz describes every one of them—his color, his nature, his wounds. Six of them were mares and from them, and those that followed, came the offspring that stocked the two Americas.

For seven hundred years in Spain the Spanish had fought off the Moors until—by adopting their mounts and their method of fighting—they conquered them and freed their home country, just as later they conquered Mexico. It is bred in their bones to be horsemen and warriors; and even yet, when they start a horse race, they use the old war cry:

"Santiago!"

Saint James was their patron saint and, when their ancestors charged the invaders, they had shouted:

"*Santiago y cierra España*—St. James and close up Spain!"

So they came and so they conquered; and, all over the New World today, wherever you find a Spaniard you will find horses and cows.

Hernando Cortés brought the first cattle to Cuba, before they were brought into Mexico; but the infiltration was slow. It was the horses that travelled ahead, and were oftenest stolen—De Soto suffering the first great loss, on the banks of the Mississippi. He had his horses picketed and side-lined, but in a night raid the Indians got them; and as the more northern Indians heard about it they stole the horses again, until they were distributed all over the West.

The Blackfeet and the Sioux had their popular heroes who travelled south thousands of miles in order to get their first horses. The Cheyennes became known as the Painted Horse People, having stolen the first Pintos; and the Nez Perces made off with Apaloosas and bred them up for war-ponies. Pinto horses were treasured on account of their bright colors and any horse with white on it was especially prized, being used to show the imprint of a bloody hand as a sign that they were on the warpath.

Among the Snake Indians the first horses were called Big Dogs. They had previously used only dogs for burden bearers and had no other name for these new beasts of burden. Horses were also called Medicine Dogs, referring to the big medicine which came from their sacred origin.

Among the Navajos, their songs to Johano-ai—the god who, riding one of his five colored horses, carries the Sun from the east to the west—seems to indicate an earlier acquaintance with them than their first meeting with the Spaniards. They went far to the east to get their first mounts and their name for the Texans is still "Iron Shirts," referring to the country where they had first seen men wearing coats of mail. "Iron Shirt" was also a common name among the northern Indians, being applied to some adventurous warrior who had killed a Spaniard while stealing horses.

Lone Wolf, the Blackfeet artist, tells the story of the first horses as it has been passed on from mouth to mouth for many generations. It is the story of a Blackfeet war party whose leader was Eagle Ribs. They went south into Always Summer Land, where the cactus grows as high as our cottonwood trees, and there saw a strange party whose warriors wore shining clothes and rode on Elk Dogs—horses.

"The story was told to me by Fish Robe, who has

gone to the land of shadows, and when I was a boy I never believed it, until I came to Arizona and saw for myself the same things. In the long ago time a bunch of about fifty warriors drifted south, passing a great salt lake and many mountains until they came to a village built on a butte, where some people worked in a garden. They sneaked up on these Indians but did not make any trouble with them, making the sign to smoke, which means peace.

"So these villagers invited the Blackfeet to come and visit them and while they were there some other Indians attacked the village. The Blackfeet put up a fight and killed some of the enemy, and for this good deed the villagers sent one of their scouts with them. After many days of travel they came to a land where cactus grows as tall as cottonwood trees, and it was where the tall cactus grows that they saw these strange people who rode Elk Dogs and wore clothes made of iron, so strong that an arrow could not shoot through them. They also had iron shields.

"When night came the Blackfeet attacked these shining warriors and killed all of them, and those were the first white men they ever saw. The Blackfeet took the Elk Dogs or horses and also some of these iron clothes, and that's how we first got the horse. Thirty or forty years ago I saw a Spanish shield belonging to a medicine bundle. When they unrolled it they said prayers and sang the song of the horse. That shield had Spanish writing on it. I must try to find out what happened to it when I go back to the Land of Plenty Snow."

For many years, among the Plains Indians, horses were the only standard of wealth. They were money and even to this day the Navajos keep thousands of wild horses, though the Government is trying to get rid of them. "Many Horses," is a favorite name among them for a man who is counted rich, and the possession of horses brings good luck.

But with the early Mexicans a horse was a god, as is shown in the story of El Morzillo, the black war horse of Cortés, when he got a splinter in his foot. On his long journey overland to Honduras Cortés encountered a branch of the great Maya tribe, and as his horse could not go on, he left him in the care of the chief, intending to come back that way. But not until a hundred years later, when two missionaries visited the lost tribe, was the fate of El Morzillo known.

As they were being shown through the grounds of the temple they came upon the image of a giant horse, crouched back on his haunches. A dozen temples, each large enough to hold a thousand men, were not sufficient to shelter all his worshippers; and the Mayas related that after Cortés left his well-beloved mount with them, they fed him on flowers, which they offered to their other gods, but the poor creature had starved to death. A great statue had been erected to El Morzillo, which the padres at once destroyed, but the people still honored his memory and refused to change their faith. Even yet the Mexican people almost worship a beautiful horse and, when the Revolution came, more than one sturdy beggar found himself mounted like a king.

Those were picked horses which, in the tiny Spanish caravels, were sent across the Atlantic to Santo Domingo and Cuba, and from there to all of Mexico and New Spain. Popular opinion has it that they were Barbs, Arabian war horses from Northern Africa, brought to Spain by the Moors to conquer the stubborn Spaniards, who after several hundred years conquered *them*. Then, with more worlds to conquer, the best horses were brought over, and Cortés began with sixteen. They were of rather light build, but extremely tough and wiry; and their direct descendants, the mustangs of the plains, have never been excelled for endurance.

When ridden by the North American Indians their sole equipment was a buffalo-skin pad and a rope tied around the lower jaw. As a hold-over from those early days the Shoshones and other northwestern tribes still mount on the off side of the horse. Holding their lances in their right hands it was easier to leap astride from that side, and in almost any relay race the northern Indians still win. But the Spaniards, though riding light, had armor for both horse and man; and, to support the rider while he thrust with his lance, the cantle of the saddle was high.

THE CONQUERORS

They rode with short stirrups, their knees bent like modern jockeys, so they could rise in the saddle and strike. Cortés ordered them to aim only at the face, as the Indians even when mortally wounded would lay hold on the shaft and drag horse and rider down. So, fighting with sword and shield as well as with lance and dagger, they cut their way through thousands of savage warriors, riding them down with their war-trained mounts.

Chapter XIV

MEXICAN RIGGING

From Mexico the Conquerors of Cortés rode south in search of more gold, until they left their mounts in Peru and all over South America. True to the tradition of the Arabs, who used only mares for war, the Spaniards always had their *manada* with them, raising colts as they went along. But in this respect the Spanish custom has changed. No *caballero* is now seen riding a mare, and it is the same all over the West. First stallions, and later geldings, were preferred, and brood mares are turned out to pasture.

As firearms took the place of sword and lance the high cantle of the Moors came down until it was lower than the horn. And the pommel was built up, to hold the turns of the *reata*, which formerly had been fastened to the cinch, or even to the horse's tail. The rope was held loose in the left hand while the right hand threw the loop, as is still the Mexican custom today; but early in the game the Texans built a saddle-horn that would *hold*. Then they tied to it, let out their stirrups, and used a much shorter rope.

The typical Texan wears high-heeled boots and uses a narrow stirrup, without *tapaderos* or toe-finders. He rides with his feet hanging straight in the saddle, hooking his stirrups with his boot-heels so that he stands with them under his instep. The high heels generally keep his feet from going through, although many a good Texan has been hung up and "drug." It is not so safe a way as the Mexican style, where the stirrups are boxed in with leather in front, often protected by heavy *tapaderos*.

But as a rule the Mexican saddles, while pretty to look at, are not as strong and serviceable as the American. In place of our steel horns and hardwood trees, they are generally made from some kind of soft wood, with a horn as big around as a soup plate. The best of these are the famous cactus-tree saddles which are made from the trunk of some giant prickly pear.

These "pears" grow along the lower Rio Grande, often reaching a height of twenty feet and branching out from a single stem. Beneath the pulpy flesh there is a woody skeleton, which with age becomes solid and very strong. The cactus trees are cut down while green and stored in some shady place until they get dried out. This takes some time, especially if the trunk is two or three feet thick, but when dried in this way they do not split.

They are then sawn out and whittled down to the desired shape, leaving the pommel very heavy for strength. These cactus trees are said to mark the beginning of the big-horn Mexican saddles, which are also made from other woods. In the most ornate, a mirror of polished silver is set on the pommel, so that the rider can look down and admire himself. But according to an old-timer, who has been with Mexicans all his life, "There ain't no 'best' among Mexican saddles—none of them are worth a damn. The leather is not cured properly and is rotten and the tree is generally made of cottonwood or some other soft wood, which has no strength. I never saw a cactus tree."

On the subject of *tapaderos,* however, this old-timer is much more lenient. In fact he says he is a *Tapadero* Man, and goes on as follows:

"The *tapaderos* used by the United States Government are short and put on the stirrup with rivets. They are to teach the soldier to ride on the ball of his foot, so he can rise up and down like the Englishman. The Chihuahua saddles have a bull-snout tap that is lined with sheepskin to keep the feet warm, and many of them highly decorated on those saddles that have the big flat horns.

"But the *tapadero* that is made for Real Cow-punchers was used in Mexico and California in the earliest days. They are about fourteen inches wide at the stirrup-crossing and twenty-four to twenty-six inches long. These a cowboy must learn to use, and when he has learned they are very helpful to his work. He becomes very expert in handling them. Throw both feet forward when running your horse in bad brush or cactus, covering his breast. It keeps off the thorns and, when a fighting cow runs into you, put your foot in front of her head. Whenever she is going to hook your horse, keep off the sharp horns.

"The *tapaderos* are made of heavy bull leather,

weighing about fourteen pounds a pair. They are also fine to ride a bronk with. After he finds he cannot kick them off he becomes gentler to other things that are brought up by his side. I used twenty-six-inch *tapaderos* and a single-cinch Visalia saddle and have saved many an old pony from being horned to death by being able to handle my taps. I use a rawhide rope and to this day am partial to a California outfit."

When we talk with an old-timer like this we realize that those long *tapaderos* are made for something beside show; and it is the same with chaparejos, or leather leggings. With the Californians, who got all their stuff from the Mexicans, the "shaps" are always closed instead of being left open behind, as with the Texans. But down in Sinaloa they use shaps which are hung on the saddle-horn, called *armas*. These are generally made of bearskin, to be worn through the heavy brush, and when the man steps off he is free of any encumbrance.

The most Mexican of all are the *tajas,* or Pancho Villa leggings, which cover the leg to above the knee and are found in Chihuahua and the northern part of the country. In the rugged mountainous regions south of the City of Mexico the real "*charro*" outfit is found, suits of soft red buckskin, and the enormous sombreros which are considered so characteristically Mexican. These are used by dancers and for gala occasions and were worn by Zapata and his outlaw followers in the mountains of Guerrero and Morelos.

They are quite as much the sign of a bandit as they are of a man working cattle; and when Porfirio Diaz undertook to put down outlawry he adopted the *charro* costume as a uniform for his Rurales, or Rural Guards. These men correspond in Mexico to the Rangers of Texas, but they were chosen in quite a different way. When a band of robbers was captured the best fighters were given the opportunity to join the Guardia Rural, instead of being killed. In this organization they were given the best horses in the country, higher pay than any of the soldiers, and the chance of continuing their old mode of life by wiping out rival bands. Since all the rest were executed on the spot there were very few who declined Don Porfirio's invitation, especially as he had been a bandit himself. They joined, and were loyal to the end, no matter who rose up against him. They were like the Swiss Guards of the French monarchs, who never betrayed their trust; and when the Revolution began they went down fighting, a gallant body of men.

The enormous sombreros serve the purpose of an umbrella in this very rainy section of the country and are said to have been made by the natives, long before the Spanish came. They are woven from the tender sprouts of any palm and are often supplemented by a cape of palm leaves, which serves the purpose of a raincoat. On the dry plains of Chihuahua the sombreros have a flat rim and, further back in the hills of Durango, the hats are woven of wheat straw,

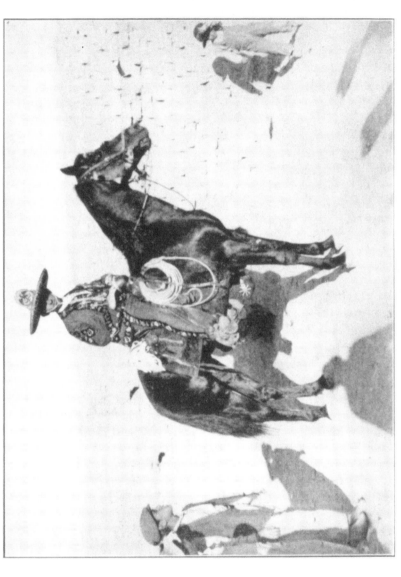

A *charro* outfit, worn on gala occasions, with the eagle and serpent of Old Mexico on the sombrero.

(Photograph by Aultman, El Paso)

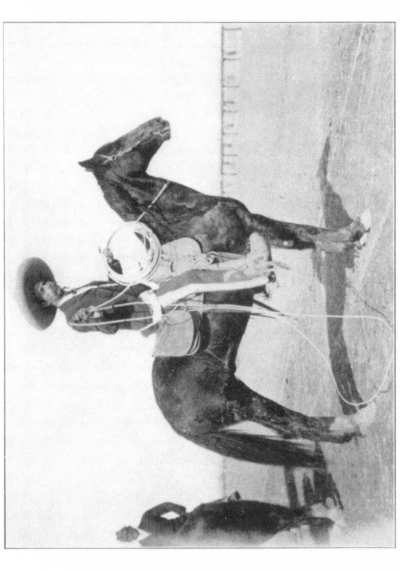

As he casts loose his coil and shakes out a loop, the Mexican gentleman becomes a cowboy, ready to make his throw.

(Photograph by Aultman, El Paso)

with a turned-up, floppy brim. In Sonora and Sinaloa the sombreros are smaller and made from the leaves of fan palms. They became widely known by the men that walked under them—the fighting Yaqui Indians.

For dress hats, felt sombreros are made, embossed with gold and silver and the eagle and serpent of Old Mexico, all beautifully done in braid. Hung over the back of their saddles they wear a *sobre jalma,* a gorgeous housing made of leopard skin or the pelt of some *tigre* cat. Bridle and spurs and stirrups are inlaid with beaten silver and, on the strings that hang down from the back of the sombrero, golden hawk-bells keep time to the horse's stride.

A Mexican *caballero* is the last word in decoration and some of the grandest wear bells on their spurs to jingle as they pass. Under the spurs on their buckskin shoes—for in a hot country they do not like boots —a double chain is suspended, to rattle on the wooden stirrups. On the outside of their Spanish bits, silver conchas are set to magnify the sound of an inside metal "cricket" which the horse spins with his tongue. A good, lively cricket can be heard half a mile and the horses seem to love their music, just as freight teams rejoice in their bell-chimes.

When it comes to "horse jewelry" the Mexicans spare no expense and, now that the Revolution has set a new style, a pair of pistols looks fine on their saddles, to match the pearl-handled gun in their belts. Every horse has a *mecate* or horsehair halter around his neck, led back to the horn and tied in a neat coil by a saddle-string. And on the right side of the saddle-bow there is a rawhide *reata,* as smooth and hard as iron, with a loop already built and ready for instant use. Like a flash the coil is cast loose from its tie-string and as he shakes out his loop the gentleman becomes a cowboy, ready to make his throw.

There are very few imitation cowboys on the ranges of Old Mexico and the regular vaqueros spend all their spare time in practicing with the *lazo.* The best roper in the world without a doubt was Oro Peso, the man who invented the art of rope-spinning, at which he has never been excelled. For years the cowboys of the West were mystified by this new stunt, many of them insisting that he had a wire through his rope which gave him that marvelous control. But Oro Peso was more than a trick roper. When he was travelling with Buffalo Bill's Wild West Show he was always posted at the gate while the cowboys and cowgirls rode their bronks, and if any were thrown and dragged by their mounts it was Oro Peso who roped them. He never failed.

Although Mexico produces the maguey-rope which the Texans generally use, the natives prefer their old-time *reatas,* made of rawhide expertly plaited. A Mexican will stick a knife and an awl into a tree knot and, using the awl for a gauge, turn a cowhide into a single string by drawing it round and round against the edge. Then the hair is trimmed off and, if made without a flaw, seven strands of this leather are twisted into a rope that will hold a mountain bull.

At making hackamores and hair bridles, and the plaited bridle reins of their long *romals*, the Mexicans are without a peer; and the best workers in stamped leather and silver are almost always of their people. It is a hereditary art, passed down from father to son, and learned originally from the Moors of Spain. As the Toledo blade set a standard for steel, so in stamped leather and silverwork the Spanish makers are best. Anyone who has gazed at the thousands of silver-mounted saddles at a typical California Rodeo will realize what an art the Mexicans have passed down to us, along with the art of horsemanship.

Chapter XV

WORKING CATTLE

WHILE in many ways the Mexicans seem rather cruel, they are really master horsemen. They have learned to break a horse and break him quick, often bringing him home "gentled" at the end of one day with a load of grass on his back. Their spade-bits and jaw-breaker ring-bits seem the last word in barbarous cruelty but they are not used until the horse is two or three years old and has been broken by the hacka-more around the nose. A well-reined Mexican horse can be guided by a touch on his neck or the move-ment of the rider's body, and in our modern Rodeo tests it is counted against a man if his mount even opens its mouth. He is supposed to rule by the touch of the reins and under no circumstances to pull the head around, as is done with an Eastern-broke horse.

The *lazo*, or lasso, was brought from Spain and is used in different forms over two continents. In Old Mexico it is generally about sixty feet long, almost al-ways of rawhide with a loop running through a reinforced *honda*, or knot. The rope is held with the knot halfway down the loop and is whirled over the head to make a throw—except in catching horses out of a corral, or in places where it will stampede the rest. Then, working on foot, it is whipped back from the ground in front and in a quick cast snapped over the head.

When the animal is down, a good roper can send a loop down the slack to snare any one of the feet, although it is a common practice to "forefoot" the horse, by catching his forefeet as he runs past. But this often results in his hip being knocked down by the fall, and the horse incapacitated for life. Many expert ropers, whose horses know they are going to get caught, can walk in on their mounts and, by a series of feints, turn them back at every break until they slip the loop over their heads.

Fifty feet is about as far as a man can throw his rope and thirty-five or forty is considered good, with the average around twenty-five feet. In throwing against the wind several loops may be held in the right hand; and there are Mexicans who can throw backwards or, like Oro Peso, make their rope do anything.

But most of the cow country in Old Mexico is rough—and much of it is also desert. In the northern and western parts, where water is scarce, the cattle are trapped by fencing in the springs or building huge corrals around the wells.

On the Seri Desert, west of Hermosillo, Sonora, where the cattle live mostly on mesquite browse, the whole range is kept under absolute control by setting a guard at each well. After three days and nights the corral gates are thrown open and the cows, rushing in to drink, are trapped by putting up the bars. Then the round-up begins in earnest, the beef cattle are cut out and the rest turned loose on the desert. This saves a lot of riding and, when the rodeo is over, every cow in the country is accounted for, with very little hard work.

There is an American style of handling cattle and a Mexican style. J. W. Fourr, Cattle Inspector at Douglas, Arizona, who has worked on both sides of the Line for fifty years, claims that the Mexicans learned their methods from the Americans. This will be news to a great many cowmen; but, since Billy was raised in Arizona and spent twenty or thirty years in Sonora, he ought to know what he is talking about and I put it down, verbatim.

"There are some very good Mexican cowboys, but they are all some that learned from the Americans. Take the crude *hombres* that came out of Old Mexico with a *zarape* wrapped around them—they could not keep up with the chuck-wagon for a week. Then they began to get on to our ways and a lot of them made good hands, but they dam sure had to learn it from us, as they did not have wild cattle to handle in their country. They would have a number of ranches and one old Don would own them all and have peons milking the cows and keeping them gentle. There was seldom a wild one and if there was one they would run it down and butcher it.

148

"Now our cowboys had to be bred and raised with wild cattle, and when the cattle business came into Texas and Colorado and the cows got into the brush or out on the plains with the buffaloes, then it was that the real cowboy work commenced. Men had to learn the dispositions and other characteristics of the cow, and the wilder she got the more they had to ride and rope. The real cowboy was first made in that New Country. The way of rounding up big countries, and roping calves and branding cattle out in the open, was done there.

"There were no corrals and the Indians were so bad that people just got their cattle branded up and left them to increase until next branding time. When I came into the picture it was a little late, but the American ways of handling cattle had been learned, and the Mexicans had to learn from the Gringo how to work cattle. The Mexicans have always built traps to catch any cattle that got a little wild. Mexican branding was always done in a corral, both in Chihuahua and Sonora.

"The round-up system is all American. Branding up calves out of a round-up is Texan. And until today a Mexican cannot drive a big herd of cattle—say fifteen hundred and up. They do not know how to string out a herd. I worked with them all my life and never saw one, old or young, that could handle big bunches. American saddles and outfits are superior in every way, just as our ways of handling horses and cattle are superior."

Well, Billy Fourr is one man who knows the cattle business, and until I meet a better man I am going to believe what he says. As long ago as 1598 Governor Oñate brought a herd of over seven thousand cattle from Zacatecas to Santa Fe, New Mexico; but that was three hundred and forty years ago, and the Mexicans have had a chance to forget. It was not until the Texans began to move their steers north—over the old Chisholm Trail and into Wyoming and Montana —that they learned the art of trailing cattle. And they still had a lot to learn when that old trail-master, Colonel Goodnight, worked out his system of making dry drives, from Texas to the Pecos River—ninety miles across the desert.

Millions of cattle were driven north through an Indian country, and before they got through, the Texans had learned their business. They had made dry drives and crossed quicksand rivers, whereas for several generations the modern Mexicans have had no great movement of cattle. Don Luis Terrazas, the greatest single cowman in the world, certainly had some big herds in Chihuahua; but it was Pancho Villa, the bandit, who rounded them up for him and put them across the Rio Grande.

In Northern Chihuahua and around Casas Grandes there were several straight Texas outfits, and Hank Smith and his bold Corralitos cowboys must have given them several lessons in the cattle business. But as long ago as 1896 I was in a part of Old Mexico where I know they handled cattle in the old way. There were only three Americans in the whole Cape Region of Baja California, and of them only one ran cows.

Chapter XVI

THE OLD WAY

IT was a land so overgrown with thorns and giant cactus that, to cut your way through it when you left the travelled trails, you had to have a cane knife or *machete*—even the little boys wore them tucked under their belts behind—and he was a brave man indeed who would even pretend to be a vaquero and ride through those terrible spines. Several of them had lost an eye. Yet I had a guide and hunter who claimed to be one of the best and, while trapping in the Sierra Laguna Mountains, I learned about their methods from him.

Gumersindo Romero had been a pearl diver at La Paz and a deer hunter at Cape San Lucas, but he was one of the few men in the country who could go out and bring in wild cattle. For this work he had a hard hat, made of rawhide, not unlike the American helmets worn in France, and the strings that held it on came down behind so he would not get hung up by the head. Over his horse's breast he tied a buckskin shield, or *pechero,* and when he went out after cattle he wore a buckskin cloak which extended to his feet.

Around his waist, like a belt, he wore his tie-down ropes; and in place of boots, he wore rawhide sandals, which he could slip off when he ran. On an open dry lake-bed I have seen him outrun a mule and head it into the corral, and doubtless he could have headed wild cows; but he preferred to go after them on a horse. Keeping watch by the water-holes he let the bunch get a big drink, to slow them down. Then he took after them through the brush, under low-hanging mesquite limbs which threatened to snake him off; until, out in some open place, he threw his *reata* over their horns and "busted" them by setting up his horse. Snatching a hogging-string from his waist he tied the steer's feet together and left him there, in that jungle of thorns and heat, while he took after the rest of the herd. Having tied down as many as he could handle, Gumersindo went back to the ranch and turned out his *cabestros*, or stalking-oxen, trained animals through whose horns a hole had been bored, to hold a wooden peg. In the horn of the wild steer a similar hole was bored—only lower down, in the quick—and the two were lashed together, tight enough so the rawhide would hold but not so it would bind. The horns were fastened in such a way that the *cabestro* could hook the steer but the steer could not hook him. Then Gumersindo rode off and left them to fight it out; and in a day or two the *cabestro* would appear, leading his victim into the corral.

This is undoubtedly the old Mexican way, as originally brought from Spain, although there are other ways. In Sinaloa, where the brush is very heavy, long lanes are cut through the trees, all leading to a big corral. Then men on foot, generally Yaqui Indians, will start a round-up through the thickets while the owner and a few horsemen will ride down the lanes, driving the cattle before them. Mexican vaqueros practically never wear boots, contenting themselves with buckskin shoes, while the foot-workers wear rawhide sandals or run through the cactus barefoot.

Bob Hiler, who has spent many years in Sonora, says the Mexican vaqueros are the best cowboys in the world when it comes to roping and riding and working over rough, rocky ground. "They will stay with it until the last cow is caught, and eat whatever grub there is without complaint. The rodeo starts at the first peep of dawn and they ride one horse all day, generally without a change, and often getting in after dark. The horses are so hardy they can stand up to it, but they are grain-fed on the spring round-up, when the grass is green and weak. They do not have to have ham and eggs for breakfast, like some of ours, to keep them from giving out."

Mexican cattle-brands are of great antiquity, going back to the Moorish *rúbricas*—signs used first as a signet or signature and later added as a flourish when the writers learned to spell out their names. Many brands are also copied from the Indian pictographs so often found on the surface of blackened rocks; and others are symbols of the sun, moon and stars. There were brand books in Spain hundreds of years ago, and in the early days in California and New Mexico such records were carefully kept. When a

In many ways the Mexicans seem cruel, but their Spanish bits are not used until the horse is two or three years old and has been broken by the hackamore around his nose.

(Photograph by Aultman, El Paso)

GUMERSINDO ROMERO.

My Baja California guide and hunter, with his .45-90 Sharps rifle. On open ground he would outrun a mule and was one of the few vaqueros in the country who could rope wild cattle in the brush.

(*Photograph by Dane Coolidge, 1896*)

horse or cow is sold, its brand is "vented"—stamped on the shoulder as a bill of sale—and the new brand burned below.

In catching wild horses many old-time tricks are used, but the ordinary way is to chase them by relays all day, keeping them away from water at night and letting them stand and get stiff. Then, after a couple of days, let them go in to some watering-place and fill up with all they can hold. After that, on fresh mounts, the horse-catchers run them down or drive them into the wings of strong corrals. It having been noted that a horse seldom looks up, they are often driven under a big tree—in the branches of which a man is concealed, who drops a loop over their heads. Or, in a flat country, if a gentle horse is tied to a tree towards which wild horses are chased, they will drift slowly over to join him and can be caught with a loop from above.

Horse races and chicken-pulls are the favorite Mexican sports, but the latter have been pretty well abolished in this country on account of their cruelty aspects. They are still favorites, however, with the Navajo and Zuni Indians, a leather strap being substituted, on state occasions, for the chicken's head.

In the old days they buried five chickens up to the neck in some sand-wash, about fifty feet apart. The rider had to run his horse over the course at a gallop, swinging down from the saddle to pull the chicken out of the sand as he passed. Oftentimes he was helped along by a quirt at the start, and when the sand was packed tight the chicken's head was all that was pulled out. In war times the Mexicans used a pistol, shooting the heads off as they passed, but before they got through, a cartridge was too valuable to be wasted.

War changed everything in Mexico and left the people miserably poor. Revolution after revolution swept over the country, each a little more destructive than the last, until most of the best horses had been driven off and the cattle killed for beef. Only when the country had been stripped of loot and the great popular leaders killed, did *El Pueblo*, the People, whom they claimed to love so much, settle down to recoup their losses.

Houses had been burned, adobe walls blasted down, the beautiful plains despoiled of their herds, and many a good vaquero, coming back from war, had to go back to raising beans. Now they are struggling up again, though still torn with bickerings and strife, and it will be many a long year before they get back to the simple life of the past.

The aristocratic *Cientificos* who once ruled the country have been driven out or killed; and a new dream, that of Equality and Justice, has risen up to take their place. Every man has been a soldier and, somewhere about his ranch, he keeps hidden the rifle or pistol that he carried during the wars. After all that has passed, the old days—as described by Burton C. Mossman, the first Captain of the Arizona Rangers and present owner of the Turkey Track Ranch in New Mexico—seems almost idyllic.

"At the old Camou Ranch, east of Camou, Sonora, I found an earthly paradise, Mexican style. The people seemed perfectly happy, they were singing all the time, and every night they had a dance. Every man had his own house and a ration of corn and beans, a garden where he could grow vegetables, and all the beef he could eat.

"The country, although covered with mesquite trees, was an absolute desert and the cattle had to come to the well to drink. This was over three hundred feet deep, big and wide and rocked with two high columns from which was supported a water-bucket. This had a wide rim of heavy iron, and was made from the entire hide of a big bull.

"An old boiler ran the engine and it hoisted five hundred pounds of water at a throw. When the rim was thrown down the hole it sank the bucket to the bottom and was immediately hoisted up again, full and bulging out round. It was dropped on a stone platform at the top, which fed the water into a big reservoir, from which it ran into two long troughs. Wood was so plentiful in that country that they had nearly a mile of fence in the corrals.

"In the daytime the cattle slept along the sand-washes under the trees, coming down at night to drink. When it was desired to catch some, a man was stationed in the brush outside the first gate, where a long wing stretched out. The wild cattle came running and horning in to water and, when they had drunk, the vaquero closed the gate and drove them into a second corral beyond. Then he would open the front gate and let a second bunch come in while he moved the others into a third corral. And so on, all night. It was easy. They could catch every cow they had.

"At the ranch, about four P.M., a boy would go out and start a fire under the boiler. Then they would throw in big sticks of mesquite wood and, when the vaqueros came in off the range, steam was up. Two men ran the pump, one at the engine and the other handling the bull-skin bucket.

"After supper the music would start up and, while the water was being raised, the people would dance by the firelight on a piece of level ground. Then they would go in, some women would sing, and they would have quartets and *corridos*. Their pay enabled them to buy chili and tobacco and clothes, and everybody seemed happy and satisfied."

THE END